The
LOUIE'S BACKYARD
Cookbook

JANE & MICHAEL STERN

WITH RECIPES BY DOUG SHOOK

THOMAS NELSON
Since 1798

NASHVILLE   DALLAS   MEXICO CITY   RIO DE JANEIRO

For our favorite parrothead,

LEWIS

Published in Nashville, Tennessee, by Thomas Nelson. Thomas Nelson is a registered trademark of Thomas Nelson, Inc.

Library of Congress Cataloging-in-Publication Data

Stern, Jane.
    The Louie's Back Yard cookbook / Jane & Michael Stern.
      p. cm.
    Includes index.
    ISBN 978-1-4016-0038-7 (hardcover)
    ISBN 978-1-4016-0513-1 (trade paper)
    1. Cookery. 2. Louie's Back Yard (Restaurant) I. Stern, Michael, 1946- II. Title.
TX714 .S773 2003
641.5—dc21
                                        2002015708

CONTENTS

FOREWORD

Coming from Washington, D.C., I didn't quite know what to expect. I was hired over the phone and arrived in Key West the day before I was to begin work. I remember walking up the steps from the lobby into the dining room and seeing for the first time the decks stepping down over the Atlantic. I said to myself, "Oh, I could stay here for awhile." That was in 1985, and now seventeen years later I stand in the same spot and tell myself the same thing. The setting is amazing with the warm climate, ocean breezes, and always magnificent skies. But a restaurant like Louie's Backyard is much more than a lovely setting.

The food at Louie's Backyard has always been extraordinary. Owners Pat Tenney and Phil Tenney are committed to providing a first-rate dining experience. They have supported me and my kitchen staff in our efforts to produce a cuisine that is unique to this place. The cuisine draws from worldwide influences yet focuses on what's *enjoyable* here, in this climate. Over the years many generous cooks have contributed the fruits of their experiences, enhancing the variety on the menus at Louie's, and the recipes in this book reflect that. While we may give the impression of laid-back islanders, the truth of the matter is that it takes very hard work to produce the wonderful food served at Louie's; but it's hard work that finds its reward in the pride we take in such a high quality finished product.

When a restaurant has been open for a number of years and has retained as much of the staff for as long as Louie's has, the biggest challenge becomes keeping the experience fresh for our customers. Everyone at Louie's Backyard, from the front door to the back, is involved in meeting that challenge on a daily basis. Whether it's searching for the best-quality ingredients, perfecting a cooking technique, or finding small ways to improve the service we give our guests, we're all growing in our capacities here.

Jane and Michael Stern, when they visited Key West to research this book, were quick to see that Louie's Backyard is the product of all of the people who have worked so hard to make it what it is. It is my hope that this book, with their observations and the recipes it contains, will capture some of the spirit of this place and allow you to bring a little of Louie's to your own backyard.

—Doug Shook

ACKNOWLEDGMENTS

What a joy it was to spend time in Paradise (a.k.a. Key West) with Doug Shook as our host. Doug is a wonder in the world of gastronomy: a man who is a great chef and also a really nice guy. Pat and Phil Tenney, co-owners of Louie's Backyard, were generous with their time and information. And we thank all the friendly, hospitable staff, cooks, and waiters alike, for opening the doorway into a restaurant that is truly one-of-a-kind.

As always when we travel, we were accompanied, in spirit, on this journey to Key West by our virtual eating partners at www.roadfood.com—Steve Rushmore Sr., Stephen Rushmore and Kristin Little, Cindy Keuchle, and Marc Bruno. They are good eaters and good friends whose enthusiasm for culinary adventure is an inspiration.

Our long-held belief in the glories of American regional cuisine has found such a satisfying expression in this series of books from the nation's most beloved restaurants. Larry Stone, Geoff Stone, Bryan Curtis, Roger Waynick, and Mike Alday are steady reminders that the Roadfood cookbooks reflect a part of America's culture that is well worth celebrating. Their steady stream of good ideas and support has made publishing a pleasure.

As always, we tip our hats in thanks to agent Doe Coover for her tireless work on our behalf, as well as to Jean Wagner, Mary Ann Rudolph, and Ned Schankman for making it possible for us to travel in confidence that all's well at home.

INTRODUCTION

A table on the three-tiered deck of Louie's Backyard is an enchanted place to dine, especially in the evening. Perched at the waterline over the Atlantic Ocean, you look out over a fathomless horizon where the clouds and waves weave together in cobalt blue striations. Hurricane lamps on the tables flicker in the calm island breeze. Bulbs strung among branches in the sheltering overhead wild hibiscus tree form a radiant canopy. Waves lap up on shore like a soft rhythm guitar that sets the tune for laughter and chat at the Afterdeck bar. There isn't a dreamier place to dine anywhere in America.

Louie's Backyard is one of many good places to eat in town, but for us it is *the* Key West restaurant. For one thing, it has been around a long time, and its roots grow deep from the fundamentals of local life. When it opened in 1971, an unknown Jimmy Buffett lived in the house next door and palled around with waiter Phil Tenney (now Louie's owner) and Chris Robinson (mixologist at Louie's Afterdeck bar). Buffett's cat Radar hung out with Robinson's dog Ten Speed; and it is said that the two of them regularly bellied up to the bar in the afternoon for broad champagne glasses filled with kahlua and cream. (Robinson remembers that Ten Speed tended to get drunk and obstreperous; Radar got extra laid-back.)

Aside from its Buffett connection and regardless of the parade of other Key

West-related celebrities who have come here to dine, Louie's demands the attention of any eater interested in discovering the unique style of cooking (and eating and serving) known as Conch cuisine.

Natives of the Florida Keys call themselves Conchs (pronounced *konks*), after the hard-shelled, spiral shellfish that is found in nearby waters, and while the term used to be derisive (like redneck or cracker), it has taken on a distinct air of pride in the last quarter century as the place that calls itself the Conch Republic has defined its cultural identity. Part of that identity is a sense of the island's unique foodways. The Conch kitchen is in some measure the progeny of nearby Cuba, of the Caribbean (both culturally and piscatorially), of Dixieland and the Cordon Bleu, but it has evolved a style all its own.

The meat of the conch itself is part of Conch cuisine (you must have conch fritters and conch chowder, not to mention raw conch salad) and so are spearfished grouper, Florida pink shrimp, Cuban picadillo, and dooryard fruit that include Key limes as well as calamondins (little, bright-flavored tangerines) and sour oranges. Conchs grow several varieties of banana, many of which are sold to creative restaurant cooks, and mango season on the island is huge. Put these ingredients together with a freewheeling kitchen spirit and the hands-on culinary education of chef Doug Shook, and you have an inevitably spectacular meal at Louie's Backyard.

What we find most enthralling about the Conch kitchen in general, but Louie's food in particular, is how much it changes day to day. The kitchen's daily repertoire reflects not only the catch of the day and what is seasonal but also the fact that Chef Shook and his kitchen team simply like to make things up as they go.

Such a devil-may-care culinary philosophy means that many of Louie's written recipes are complex. The kind of creativity expressed in this book is not one that spawns quickie meals and kitchen shortcuts. While not necessarily difficult, the style of cooking embodied in Louie's recipes is one for people who enjoy the entire process of creating a meal, from procuring the ingredients to making a handsome presentation of a finished dish.

Doug later explained to us, "The specials are about seeing what you have and imagining the best thing to do with it. Earlier today, I walked around the kitchen holding one of those pink snappers, half in a daze, thinking what I could do with it. For me, it is all about making it up as I go along."

There you have the spirit of Louie's Backyard. Some elements about the dining experience are predictable: the spectacular view over the ocean and the expertly concocted margaritas and piña coladas served forth by bartender Chris Robinson. But when it comes to eating a meal, all you know for sure is that it will be colorful, high-flavored, and Conch in character.

THE BACKYARD RESTAURANT

The seaside home in which Louie's Backyard cooks and serves meals was built a hundred years ago by James Randall Adams, a sailing captain who made his fortune in the wrecking industry. Now listed on the National Register of Historic Places, Adams' house was designed in a kind of Conch/Greek revival style with Doric columns, Bahamian shutters, and a two-story porch. The captain was proud to say that nearly all its furnishings, even the dishware, was salvage he had collected from ships run aground.

The house passed through several hands during the twentieth century. In the 1970s it was owned by Frances and Louie Signorelli. Louie was known as an excellent host and cook; and in 1971 he was encouraged by his friends to open a five-table restaurant in the backyard overlooking the Atlantic Ocean. He had one waiter and he cooked about a dozen meals each night out of his own kitchen; his cash register was a cigar box.

When Louie started serving food to the public, there wasn't a big dining scene in Key West. Drinking, yes; the town now known as Margaritaville has long provided plenty of opportunity to sit on a barstool and "solve" the world's problems. Thirty years ago, however, the choice of

Just a few blocks from the Southernmost Point, Louie's Backyard exudes a neighborly friendliness that is both inviting and relaxing.

places to eat well on the island was slim. There was a raw bar and a lobster house and a couple of aspiring French restaurants. At that time the idea of a vibrant Key West culinary style hadn't begun to crystallize.

Creating Conch cuisine was not Louie Signorelli's goal. Phil Tenney, who was that single waiter in the early days and is now co-owner of Louie's, remembers that "We did a kind of fine dining, but a different kind of fine dining, using seafood from the Key West waters and serving it in a casual atmosphere, but an atmosphere with the nicest ambience." Phil remembers that subsequent owner Walter Perry came up with a rather ambiguous motto that somehow fit: *An inexpensive place for people who have money.*

Louie's oceanside setting is awesome, but it is not austere. There is a neighborly friendliness about the old house just a few blocks from the southernmost point in the continental U.S. that sets it apart from those restaurants more centrally located in bustling business-district areas of Key West. The sight of the far-off horizon and the sound of waves lapping on the

The Afterdeck at Louie's juts out over the Atlantic, providing a magnificent view and a unique dining experience.

sand are complemented by the sights and sounds of the small beach that adjoins the restaurant, a place known as Dog Beach because it is the only spot on the island where people are welcome to swim and frolic with their dogs. Sporting dogs splash and paddle in the water and step out onto the beach to furiously shake themselves dry. Landbound pooches play Frisbee with their human companions or just dig holes in the sand.

From the beginning, the restaurant's exquisite location and the culinary talents of Louie himself seemed to make this location fertile ground for the kind of extraordinarily creative cooking that gives birth to new dishes and to a whole new style of food. After Louie Signorelli came the celebrated Chef Norman Van Aken, who honed his talents during four years at the helm of the kitchen, creating what he called *Nuevo Cubano* cuisine. Van Aken established recipes for a few of Louie's specialties that are still on the menu: hot fried chicken salad, conch chowder, and conch fritters. During Van Aken's tenure, the young Charlie Trotter spent a season in the kitchen.

Louie's fell onto hard times in the late 1970s and closed for a few years until Phil and Pat Tenney bought the place in 1982. They did a major physical restoration, but having been a waiter in Louie's early days, Phil knew that he wanted to continue the same Conch spirit of the place that Louie Signorelli had instilled in its earliest days. "I remember when Louie opened up. He served crudités, bagna cauda, snapper throats," Phil says. "It was a simple menu, with only three or four entrées such as New Zealand lamb and local fish, but everything was prepared with care and skill." Doug Shook's arrival in 1985 signaled a new era of culinary diversity, but Louie's original devotion to a menu that was casual and friendly and to food that honestly expressed regional taste has never wavered.

And so, for all its sophistication, Louie's Backyard remains a decidedly local restaurant. Phil Tenney recalls, "By the time we opened up in '83, the navy had pulled out of Key West, and a lot of free-spirited types had moved in. There had always been a lot of bars here, but good places to eat had been scarce. We became a restaurant to which locals came like it belonged to them; many made it a kind of second home. Visitors to Key West who had any sense of fine dining felt they *had to* come to Louie's at least once during their stay. And that's the way it has been ever since."

BREAKFAST

Buttermilk Biscuits

Croissant French Toast

"Lost Bread"

Louie's Granola

Poached Eggs on Sourdough Toast

Smoked Lobster Benedict

Lobster Quiche

Sweet Corn Fritters

BUTTERMILK BISCUITS

These are really, really good biscuits. They come from a house recipe used since 1985, from Susan Porter, Louie's original pastry chef.

2	*cups all-purpose flour*
4	*teaspoons baking powder*
½	*teaspoon salt*
2	*teaspoons sugar*
½	*teaspoon cream of tartar*
¼	*teaspoon baking soda*
½	*cup unsalted butter, cold, cut into ½-inch cubes*
¾	*cup buttermilk*

Preheat the oven to 400°F. Combine the flour, baking powder, salt, sugar, cream of tartar, and baking soda in the work bowl of a food processor and pulse the machine a few times to mix everything together well. Add the butter and pulse the machine again until the butter is cut into pea-sized pieces. With the machine running, pour the buttermilk in through the feed tube. Stop the machine as soon as the dough comes together. Turn the biscuit dough out onto a lightly floured board and knead gently about a dozen times. Roll the dough out into a 9 x 16-inch rectangle, fold the dough in thirds, and roll out again to a 1-inch thickness. Cut the dough into rounds with a floured 3-inch cutter. Transfer to a baking sheet. Gather the scraps and reroll them until all of the dough has been rolled and cut. Bake the biscuits for 12 minutes or until they are high and golden brown. Serve warm.

MAKES ABOUT 8 BISCUITS

CROISSANT FRENCH TOAST
with Berries and Chocolate-Peanut Butter Sauce

This is an invention of Pat Tenney's and it's as good, as rich, as inner-child-fulfilling as it sounds.

4	large, day-old croissants	**CHOCOLATE SAUCE:**	
4	extra large eggs	3	ounces bittersweet chocolate, cut into small chunks
½	teaspoon ground cinnamon	3	ounces smooth, country-style peanut butter
1	teaspoon vanilla extract		
1	cup half-and-half	1	ounce light corn syrup
2	plus 2 tablespoons butter	2	ounces heavy cream or half-and-half
BERRIES:			
2	cups fresh red raspberries		
1	cup fresh blueberries		

Split the croissants in half lengthwise. Beat the eggs well with the cinnamon, vanilla, and half-and-half. Heat 2 tablespoons of the butter in a wide cast iron or non-stick skillet. Dip 4 of the croissant halves in the egg mixture and place them cut side down in the skillet. Cook for about 3 minutes or until the bottoms are nicely browned and then turn the pieces over and brown the other side. Remove the croissant pieces to a paper towel-lined plate and repeat with the remaining pieces.

For the berries, place the raspberries in a blender and purée until smooth. Strain the purée through a medium sieve to remove the seeds if desired. Stir the blueberries into the raspberry purée.

To make the chocolate sauce, combine the chocolate, peanut butter, corn syrup, and cream in a small bowl and place it over a pot of simmering water. Cook on medium-low, stirring occasionally, until the chocolate has melted and the sauce is smooth and creamy. Keep the sauce warm.

To serve, cover the bottoms of four large plates with the berry mixture. Arrange 2 croissant halves cut side up over the berry sauce and drizzle 2 to 3 tablespoons of the chocolate sauce over them. Pass the remaining berries and chocolate sauce separately.

MAKES 4 SERVINGS

"LOST BREAD"

This is savory, stuffed French Toast, or Pain Perdu. It's rich and cheesy and really good. Shrimp can replace the ham in the filling, and other firm cheeses can be used.

2	*cups grated white Cheddar*
4	*tablespoons all-purpose flour*
2	*extra large eggs*
1	*plus 6 extra large egg yolks*
1	*teaspoon sea salt*
⅛	*teaspoon cayenne*
1	*cup diced boiled ham*
2	*tablespoons chopped Italian parsley*
8	*slices sturdy white bread, crusts removed, cut into 4-inch circles*
2	*cups half-and-half*
	Sea salt
	Freshly ground black pepper
2	*tablespoons butter*
8	*tablespoons sour cream, for garnish*
4	*tablespoons sliced scallions, for garnish*

Preheat the oven to 400°F. To make the filling, combine the cheese and flour in the work bowl of a food processor. Process briefly to combine them; then, with the motor running, add the eggs, one at a time, and the 1 egg yolk. Process to a smooth paste and add the salt and cayenne. Transfer the mixture to a small bowl and stir in the ham and parsley. Divide the filling among 4 of the bread slices, spreading it evenly edge to edge. Cover the filling with the remaining 4 bread slices. Beat the remaining 6 egg yolks with the half-and-half and salt and pepper to taste. Dip each sandwich in the egg mixture, making sure that all of the bread becomes saturated. Heat the butter in a wide, ovenproof skillet and when it is foaming, carefully add the sandwiches. Cook for 2 minutes until the bottoms are nicely browned and then turn them over. Place the skillet in the oven for 8 to 10 minutes, or until the second sides are also browned and the filling is bubbly. Place each "lost bread" in the center of a plate and top with the sour cream and scallions.

MAKES 4 SERVINGS

LOUIE'S GRANOLA

We serve this for brunch topped with mixed fresh berries and sheep's milk yogurt from The Old Chatham Sheepherding Co. in New York, which is so tangy and fresh it's like tasting yogurt for the first time. Of course, regular yogurt is good, too.

4½	cups old-fashioned oats
3	cups sliced almonds
3	cups hulled pumpkin seeds
1	cup canola oil
¼	cup honey
½	cup maple syrup
1	tablespoon pure vanilla extract
1½	tablespoons ground cinnamon
⅛	teaspoon ground cloves
1½	teaspoons sea salt
1	cup golden raisins
1	cup dried sour cherries
1	cup dried star fruit
1	cup Zante currants (any currant will do)

Preheat the oven to 300°F. Mix the oats, almonds, and pumpkin seeds together in a large bowl. Combine the oil, honey, syrup, vanilla, cinnamon, cloves, and salt in a small saucepan and cook over medium heat, stirring often, until the mixture boils and comes together. Pour the oil mixture over the oats and toss to coat everything well. Spread the mixture out on two rimmed cookie sheets and bake, stirring and turning every 10 minutes, for 30 to 40 minutes or until the mixture is browned and crisp. Remove the pans from the oven and allow the mixture to cool. Transfer the mixture to a large bowl, mix in the raisins, cherries, star fruit, and currants and store at room temperature in Ziploc bags or jars with tight-fitting lids.

MAKES ABOUT 15 CUPS

POACHED EGGS ON SOURDOUGH TOAST
with Tomatoes, Greens, and Crispy Prosciutto

An Eggs Benedict update: The sliced prosciutto becomes crispy, like bacon, and the extra-lemony hollandaise dresses the bitter greens as well as the eggs.

4	*slices prosciutto di Parma (see note), about 3 x 7 inches, paper thin*
2	*tablespoons fresh lemon juice*
2	*cups Hollandaise Sauce (page 104)*
2	*quarts water*
2	*tablespoons distilled white vinegar*
8	*extra large eggs*
1	*bunch arugula, stems removed, washed, and dried*
1	*bunch watercress, tough stems removed, washed, and dried*
4	*slices sourdough bread, at least ½ inch thick, toasted*
2	*small, red, ripe tomatoes, cored and sliced ½ inch thick (8 slices)*

Preheat the oven to 400°F. Lay the slices of prosciutto on a parchment-lined baking pan and place the pan in the oven for 10 to 12 minutes or until the prosciutto is very crisp. Transfer the prosciutto to a plate. Stir the lemon juice into the Hollandaise Sauce. Bring the water and vinegar to a boil. Reduce the heat to a simmer. Break each egg into a small bowl and slip the egg into the water. Poach the eggs for 3 to 4 minutes. Carefully remove the eggs to a paper towel-lined plate to drain.

To serve, mix the arugula and watercress together and divide them among four plates. Place a slice of sourdough toast in the center of each plate. Top the toast with 2 slices of tomato. Place an egg on each tomato slice and coat the eggs with the hollandaise. Drizzle some of the sauce over the greens too. Crumble a slice of prosciutto over the egg on each plate and serve.

MAKES 4 SERVINGS

Note: Domestic prosciutto would be acceptable, or even Smithfield ham as long as the slices are very thin.

SMOKED LOBSTER BENEDICT
with Orange Hollandaise

This is deluxe. Smoking the lobster adds a complexity to the flavors, but it isn't essential. The lobster could be wrapped in plastic, cooked in boiling water for nine minutes, and then shelled and cut into pieces.

2	(6-ounce) Florida lobster tails, split, shelled, and deveined	2	cups Hollandaise Sauce (page 104)
4	tablespoons plus 1 cup fresh orange juice	2	quarts water
4	tablespoons fresh lime juice	2	tablespoons white distilled vinegar
1	tablespoon soy sauce	8	extra large eggs
2	tablespoons canola oil	4	Buttermilk Biscuits (page 7)
	Soaked hickory chips	2	tablespoons snipped fresh chives, for garnish

Light a small charcoal fire in a drum-style smoker. While the coals are burning down, marinate the lobster tail meat with the 4 tablespoons orange juice, the lime juice, soy sauce, and canola oil. When the coals are ready, add the soaked hickory chips to the fire and put the lobster on the grate in the smoker. Cover and smoke for 12 to 15 minutes or until the lobster is just cooked through. Remove the lobster from the smoker and when it is cool enough to handle, cut it into ½ -inch slices. Bring the 1 cup orange juice to a boil and reduce to ¼ cup. Stir the reduced orange juice into the hollandaise. Bring the water and white vinegar to a boil. Reduce the heat to a simmer. Break each egg into a small bowl and slip the egg into the water. Poach the eggs for 3 to 4 minutes. Carefully remove the eggs to a paper towel-lined plate to drain.

To serve, split the biscuits and place them cut side up on four plates. Top each biscuit half with slices of smoked lobster. Place the poached eggs over the lobster and coat the eggs generously with the orange-flavored hollandaise. Garnish with the snipped chives and serve.

MAKES 4 SERVINGS

Phil Tenney, Co-Owner

Phil Tenney, who is now co-owner of Louie's Backyard with his ex-wife Pat, was the first waiter to work at the restaurant when it opened in 1971. Phil had come to Key West early that year with actor Lloyd Bridges to work on a TV series called *Let's Go Boating.* "We were all hippies in those days," he recalls. "We had long hair down our backs. It was an anything-goes time. My passion then, as it is now, was woodworking. From 1973 to 1983, I ran a wood shop. I went to Belize and got the wood, and I did a lot of the woodwork that is still here at the restaurant: the bars, inside and out, the wood statues."

Phil and Pat bought Louie's Backyard in 1982 after it had been closed for more than five years. They restored the old house and opened up with a menu that reflected the restaurant that Louie Signorelli had started ten years earlier. "We tried to maintain the spirit of the original," Phil says. "A simple menu with local fish and New Zealand lamb and good margaritas. We don't go for the foo-foo drinks here. Those you get down there, on Duval Street."

LOBSTER QUICHE
with Spinach and Roasted Peppers

Lobster, fresh spinach, and roasted peppers are luxurious ingredients, which make a delicious quiche. We make many varieties of quiche but always with the same crust, the layer of sweet stewed onions, and the very rich custard of cream and egg yolks. With support like that any ingredient that's added seems luxurious.

QUICHE SHELL:

1½	cups all-purpose flour
¾	cup cold, unsalted butter, cut into ¼-inch cubes
½	teaspoon sea salt
¼	cup ice water

FILLING:

1	tablespoon butter
1	tablespoon canola oil
1	large yellow onion, peeled and thinly sliced
1	pound fresh spinach, stems removed and washed
2	(6-ounce) Florida lobster tails, in the shell
6	extra large egg yolks
2	cups heavy cream
	Sea salt
	Freshly ground black pepper
	Freshly grated nutmeg
1	red or yellow bell pepper, roasted, peeled, seeded, and cut into ¼-inch strips
2	cups grated Gruyere cheese

For the quiche shell, put the flour, butter, and salt in the work bowl of a food processor and pulse the mixture until it resembles small crumbs. With the machine running, add the ice water a tablespoon at a time. Stop the machine as soon as the dough begins to come together. Gather the dough into a ball, flatten it into a disk, wrap it in plastic wrap, and refrigerate it for at least 30 minutes. Preheat the oven to 350°F. Roll the dough out into a 15-inch circle. Carefully transfer the dough to a deep, 10-inch quiche pan with a removable bottom. Trim the edges flush with the edge of the pan. Line the pastry with a sheet of foil or parchment, fill it half full with rice or dried beans, and place it in the oven for 18 minutes. Remove the weights and the foil and continue baking for 7 minutes longer, until the shell is lightly browned.

For the filling, heat the butter and canola oil in a small saucepan, add the sliced onions, and stir to coat them well. Cover the pan, lower the heat to very low, and cook the onions very slowly, stirring occasionally, for 45 minutes or until they are very sweet and tender. Remove the cover, raise the heat to medium, and cook for 10 minutes longer to evaporate most of the liquid in the pan. Don't let the onions brown. Place the spinach, still wet from being washed, in a covered pan large enough to hold it. Place the pan over medium high heat and cook, covered for 10 minutes, until the spinach is wilted and hot. Drain the spinach, rinse it under cool running water, and squeeze it as dry as possible in a kitchen towel. Wrap the lobster tails tightly in several layers of plastic wrap. Bring 2 quarts of water to a boil in a large saucepan. Add the lobster tails and cook for exactly 6 minutes. Transfer the lobster tails to a bowl of ice water and cool them completely. Remove the plastic wrap and take the lobster meat from the shell. Cut it into 1-inch pieces. The lobster meat will not be completely cooked at this point.

Beat the egg yolks with the heavy cream. Season the mixture to taste with salt, pepper, and nutmeg.

To assemble the quiche, spread the onions in an even layer over the bottom of the shell. Separate the spinach and spread it out over the onions. Scatter the lobster evenly over the spinach and do the same with the roasted red pepper strips. Add the grated cheese in an even layer. Pour in the egg mixture, stopping when it reaches to ¼ inch below the edge of the crust.

Bake in the oven for 1¼ hours or until the quiche is just set in the center. Let it cool and settle for at least 15 minutes before slicing.

MAKES 8 SERVINGS

Pat Tenney, Co-Owner

After arriving in Key West in the early 1970s, Pat Tenney found herself working at the original Louie's Backyard. She was not only a waitress but also brought in Louie's desserts, which she baked at home. "There were a lot of big changes that happened in Key West in the 1970s," she recalls. "A lot of renovation, a lot of building." She didn't set out to own a restaurant, but "when we bought the old place in '82, it was a good time to give it new life."

Pat and her then-husband Phil added the back half of the restaurant as well as the decks heading out towards the ocean. It was a yearlong project that in some ways, for Pat, has never ended. The distinctive *look* of Louie's is Pat's primary ongoing responsibility. "It's all her," Doug says. "She is constantly upgrading the property: new chairs, new rugs, artwork, a whole new Brazilian walnut floor. She has a real flair for that, and the restaurant reflects her vision."

"I like to change things," she says. "As I see it, Louie's Backyard is a work in progress and I hope it always will be. When you stay the same, you become status quo and you become boring—for the staff and the customers." She points out that because it is far from Duval Street, where most of the island's commerce is centered, the restaurant needs to have the kind of personality that makes it a destination off the beaten path.

Whatever changes Pat makes to the décor, the ambience remains constant: an easy-to-like Key West attitude that she calls "casual elegance." Louie's character never could have been created by a corporate committee or maintained by a franchisee. "This is a very personal spot, for me and for so many of us who have been involved with it," she emphasizes. "As we change, so does the restaurant."

SWEET CORN FRITTERS
with Maple Syrup and Country Ham

Here is a bit of the South from the Southernmost Brunch.

6	*ears fresh sweet corn, husks removed*
3	*extra large eggs, separated*
1	*cup all-purpose flour*
2	*teaspoons baking powder*
1	*teaspoon sea salt*
1	*teaspoon sugar*
½	*teaspoon Tabasco*
	Canola oil for frying
6	*slices country ham*
1½	*cups pure maple syrup, warmed*

Remove the corn kernels from the cobs with a sharp knife, and scrape the cobs with the back of the knife to extract as much milk and pulp as possible. Place the corn kernels in a food processor and pulse a few times to roughly chop them. Add the egg yolks and pulse again to distribute them evenly. Sift the flour, baking powder, salt, and sugar together into a mixing bowl. Add the corn and Tabasco and stir well to combine them. In a separate bowl beat the egg whites until they form stiff peaks and gently fold them into the corn. Heat at least 2 inches of canola oil in a wide, deep pot or deep-fat fryer to 375°F. Drop tablespoonfuls of the fritter batter into the oil and cook for about 2 minutes before turning to brown the other side. Drain the fritters on paper towels.

To serve, place a slice of country ham on each of six plates. Arrange the fritters around the ham and pour the syrup over everything.

MAKES 6 SERVINGS

APPETIZERS

Chilled Gulf Shrimp

Chilled Spicy Shrimp

Portobello Mushroom Carpaccio

Sirloin Carpaccio

Crab and Corn Gratin

Blue Crab Cakes

Crisp Fried Marinated Shrimp

Mussels Steamed in Coconut Milk

Cavatelli

Cavatelli with Shrimp

Grilled Gulf Shrimp and Chorizo

Chorizo

Conch Fritters

Grilled Prosciutto-Wrapped Shrimp

Seared Sea Scallops

Timbales of Brioche and Smoked Trout

Mussels Steamed in White Wine

Chicken Saté

Mango Slaw

Spiedini of Beef

Fried Fresh Calamari

Littleneck Clams

Citrus-Cured Rainbow Trout

CHILLED GULF SHRIMP
with Cucumber Ribbons and Papaya-Chili Ice

This dish is as cool and refreshing as its name implies, with sharp, bright flavors to cut through the heat of a Key West afternoon.

8	cups water
24	extra large Gulf shrimp
1	English cucumber
1	small bell pepper, red or yellow

PAPAYA-CHILE ICE:

2	very ripe papayas, peeled and seeded
2	tablespoons fresh lime juice
½	cup light corn syrup
1	tablespoon chili paste with garlic

DRESSING:

¼	cup fresh lime juice
¼	cup Thai fish sauce
¼	cup water
1	tablespoon rice vinegar
2	teaspoons sugar
1	clove garlic, finely chopped
1	pinch of crushed red pepper flakes
½	cup cilantro or mint leaves, for garnish

In a large pot bring the water to a boil. Add the shrimp and cook them for 2½ minutes. Drain the shrimp and refrigerate until cool. Peel and devein the shrimp and cut them in half lengthwise. Refrigerate. Cut the cucumber into 1-inch-wide ribbons with a Benriner spiral cutter or with a swivel-bladed vegetable peeler. Seed and finely dice the bell pepper.

To make the Papaya-Chile Ice, combine the papaya pulp in the work bowl of a food processor with the lime juice, corn syrup, and chili paste. Process to a smooth purée. Freeze the mixture in an ice cream maker according to the manufacturer's directions.

To serve, toss the cucumber ribbons with the diced bell pepper and place them in wide martini glasses or small bowls. Arrange the chilled shrimp over the cucumbers. Mix the dressing ingredients in a jar with a tight-fitting lid and shake well. Spoon 2 tablespoons of the dressing evenly over each portion and place a scoop of papaya ice in the center. Garnish with the cilantro or mint leaves.

MAKES 6 TO 8 SERVINGS

CHILLED SPICY SHRIMP
with Rum-Soaked Golden Pineapple

Golden pineapple from Costa Rica is so sweet and juicy it almost doesn't need embellishment. The Falernum in the marinade is a spiced sugar syrup made in the West Indies, and can be hard to find. It can be omitted.

SHRIMP:

1	onion, peeled and sliced
2	ribs celery, cut into 1-inch pieces
2	carrots, peeled and cut into 1-inch pieces
1	bay leaf
1	tablespoon whole black peppercorns
2	quarts water
2	pounds (about 36) extra large pink Gulf shrimp

SPICY MARINADE:

4	tablespoons Chinese chili paste with garlic
4	tablespoons roasted sesame oil
4	tablespoons rice wine vinegar
4	tablespoons brown sugar
2	teaspoons white sesame seeds
2	teaspoons black sesame seeds
1	tablespoon soy sauce
½	cup diced red bell pepper
4	tablespoons chopped fresh cilantro

PINEAPPLE:

1	golden pineapple
3	tablespoons fresh orange juice
3	tablespoons fresh lemon juice
3	tablespoons fresh lime juice
¼	cup Myers's rum
¼	cup falernum
½	whole nutmeg, grated
	Whole fresh cilantro leaves

Combine the onion, celery, carrots, bay leaf, peppercorns, and water in a deep pot and bring to a boil. Cook for 10 minutes and then add the shrimp. Cook for exactly 3 minutes. Drain the shrimp in a colander, discarding the vegetables and cooking liquid. Chill the shrimp and, when cool, peel and devein them, leaving the tail shells intact.

To make the marinade, combine the chili paste, sesame oil, rice wine vinegar, brown sugar, white and black sesame seeds, soy sauce, red bell pepper, and cilantro in a small bowl.

To prepare the pineapple, after removing the skin and the "eyes," cut the fruit into quarters lengthwise, removing the central core. Cut each quarter into thin lengthwise slices. Place them in a flat dish. Combine the orange, lemon, and lime juices with the rum, falernum, and nutmeg and pour the mixture over the pineapple. Refrigerate for at least one hour before serving.

To serve, divide the pineapple slices among six appetizer plates. Toss the shrimp with the spicy marinade to coat them well and arrange them on the plates with the pineapple. Garnish with whole cilantro leaves.

MAKES 6 SERVINGS

PORTOBELLO MUSHROOM CARPACCIO
with Herbed Chèvre and Sun-Dried Tomatoes

These mushrooms are so attractive when they've been pounded and flattened that it almost seems a shame to cover them up, but the herbed cheese and tomatoes are a perfect complement.

CARPACCIO:

6	large portobello mushroom caps, about 4 inches in diameter
¾	cup olive oil

HERBED CHÈVRE:

6	ounces chèvre, at room temperature
6	ounces cream cheese, room temperature
2	teaspoons finely chopped fresh garlic
1	tablespoon fresh thyme leaves
1	tablespoon snipped fresh chives
1	teaspoon grated lemon zest
½	teaspoon freshly ground black pepper
3	cups mixed baby greens
6	sun-dried tomatoes packed in olive oil, drained
1	tablespoon walnut oil
2	teaspoons champagne vinegar

To make the carpaccio, brush each mushroom cap liberally with olive oil and place stem side up on a small baking pan. Place the pan in a 350°F oven for 15 minutes until the mushrooms are hot and softened. Remove the mushrooms from the oven and allow them to cool. Place a 12-inch square of parchment paper or plastic wrap on a work surface and center a mushroom cap on it right side up. Cover with a second piece of paper or plastic wrap. With the smooth side of a meat mallet or the bottom of a small, heavy pan, smack the mushroom cap to flatten it into a circle about 8 or 9 inches in diameter. Use enough force to break the flesh of the mushroom and

gradually flatten it, but not enough to pulverize it. Repeat with the remaining mushroom caps.

For the herbed chèvre, combine the chèvre with the cream cheese, garlic, thyme, chives, lemon zest, and pepper and mix them together well. Chill the herbed chèvre in the refrigerator.

To serve, carefully remove the parchment paper or plastic wrap from the bottom, or darker side, of one of the mushroom caps. Lay the mushroom on a plate and remove the top piece of parchment. Repeat with the remaining mushrooms. Divide the chèvre into six equal portions and place one portion in the center of each mushroom carpaccio. Toss the mixed greens with the tomatoes, oil, and vinegar and place them in a compact little pile over the chèvre.

MAKES 6 SERVINGS

SIRLOIN CARPACCIO
with Capers, Truffle Oil, and Parmesan

There are only four components of this dish—none of them cooked—but the mingling of flavors provide a tasting experience that's memorable.

1½   *pounds (1½ inches thick) prime sirloin, trimmed and cut into 6 pieces*

4   *tablespoons Italian white truffle oil*

2   *tablespoons capers, drained*

1   *(4-ounce) piece Parmigiano-Reggiano*

Place a 12-inch square of parchment paper on a work surface and center a piece of sirloin on it. Cover with a second piece of parchment. With the flat side of a meat mallet or the bottom of a small heavy pot, pound the meat until it is 8 to 10 inches in diameter and paper thin. Take care not to tear the meat. Repeat with the remaining pieces of sirloin. Remove one of the pieces of paper, lay the carpaccio on a large dinner plate and remove the second piece of paper. Repeat with the remaining portions. Drizzle 2 teaspoons of the truffle oil evenly over each carpaccio. Scatter 1 teaspoon capers over the meat. With a swivel-bladed vegetable peeler, shave curls of the Parmesan onto each plate and serve.

MAKES 6 SERVINGS

CRAB AND CORN GRATIN
with Roasted Red Pepper Rouille

A family vacation in North Carolina where the Silver Queen corn grows near the estuaries full of blue crabs inspired this summertime dish. Only very fresh corn will do, with bright green vibrant husks and pale golden silk.

CORN:

2	*ears fresh sweet corn*
3	*cups cream*
1	*large shallot, peeled and finely chopped*
1	*teaspoon sea salt*
¼	*teaspoon cayenne*
¼	*teaspoon celery seeds (optional)*

GRATINS:

2	*pounds jumbo lump crabmeat, picked over for pieces of shell and cartilage*
1	*cup fresh breadcrumbs*
3	*tablespoons cold butter, cut into ¼-inch pieces*
1	*cup Red Pepper Rouille (page 108)*

For the corn, shuck the ears and with a sharp knife cut the kernels from the cobs. Set the kernels and the corncobs aside separately. Bring 4 cups of salted water to a boil over high heat, add the corn kernels, and cook them for 4 minutes. Drain in a colander and set aside. In a deep pot combine the cream, shallots, and the corncobs. Bring to a boil and reduce the heat so the cream just simmers; cook for 12 to 15 minutes, stirring to keep the corncobs from sticking and scorching, or until the cream is reduced by half. Remove the corncobs and set them aside on a plate to cool. When the corncobs are cool enough to handle scrape them with the back of a knife to remove all of the corn pulp and the cream that is clinging to them. Return this "paste" to the pot with the reduced cream and discard the corncobs. Season the corn with salt, cayenne, and celery seeds, if using.

For the gratins, preheat the oven to 400°F. Combine the crabmeat with the cream and the cooked corn kernels. Taste for seasoning. Divide the mixture among 8 small gratin dishes or spread it out in one large, wide casserole. Sprinkle the breadcrumbs over the crabmeat and dot the top with the pieces of butter. Bake the gratins for 12 to 15 minutes, until hot and bubbling and nicely browned on top. Drizzle 1 tablespoon of the Red Pepper Rouille over each gratin and serve very hot.

MAKES 8 SERVINGS

The Conch Republic

The trip along Route 1 from Miami to Key West skims over sky-blue sea, past breeze-swept mangroves, as it leaves the mundane rules and regulations of the USA behind. When you get to Mile Marker 0, you are a world away from life as we know it everywhere else in America. You are 150 miles from Miami, but less than 100 miles from Cuba. Being at the end of the line—as far as you can go along Route 1—has helped foster a libertine attitude in this place. As far back as the early nineteenth

The libertine attitude fosters all sorts of entertainment.
Photo courtesy of Florida Keys TDC.

century, Key West's success had a dubious foundation. It was then known as the wrecking capital of the world, meaning that its original Bahamian settlers figured out how to make fortunes by salvaging cargo from vessels that had run aground on the coral reefs off the Florida Keys. Admiralty Court law required that all goods taken from wrecked ships in the area go through Key West, and by 1830, the tiny town had become the wealthiest city per capita in the United States.

Key West was the largest city in Florida before the Civil War, and, always of an independent mind, it was one of the only southern cities to remain loyal to the Union during the Civil War. In the late nineteenth century it enjoyed success again when Cuban cigar makers temporarily—they eventually moved to Tampa—found refuge from the tyranny of Spain. In 1912, with the completion of the Overseas Railroad—a railroad constructed across 128 miles of rock islands and open water—Key West was finally connected to the mainland as it had never been before. The railroad, built by Henry Flagler's Florida East Coast Railroad, made Key West America's largest deepwater port on the Atlantic coast south of Norfolk, Virginia. Trade increased, and Key West flourished for twenty-three years, recovering from the loss of the cigar industry. Then, in 1935 a devastating hurricane hit the Upper and Middle Keys, destroying much of Flagler's railroad at

The Overseas Highway.
<small>Photo courtesy of Florida Keys TDC.</small>

the height of the Great Depression, and the former boomtown became America's poorest city.

The Overseas Highway was built in 1938 (using much of the old railroad bed), reconnecting Key West to the rest of America, but it wasn't until the reactivation of the Key's naval base during World War II that the infusion of government money put the town back on its feet.

Reestablished as a tourist resort with the patina of famous visitors and citizens (Hemingway, Wallace Stevens, Robert Frost), Key West became a destination for vacationers in search of sun, warmth, and deep-sea fishing. In April 1982 the U.S. Border Patrol started searching everyone who traveled from the Keys to the mainland for illegal immigrants. The citizens of Key West, furious with the Feds for violating their freedom, seceded from the Union. Calling themselves "Conchs," an old derisive term for island natives, the

rebellious populace launched a salvo of stale Cuban bread and declared themselves separate and apart from the United States of America. The blockade was abandoned, but the Conch Republic that declared its independence during that playful revolution endures. Formally of course, Key West remains part of the United States, but for many who love it with patriotic zeal, the Conch Republic is a virtual nation with an insouciant culture like no place else.

For many people, Key West today *is* Margaritaville. That is how Jimmy Buffet put it when, as legend has it, he fell out of his hammock one morning in 1971 when he was living on the beach next to Louie's Backyard. He stumbled over to the Afterdeck Bar and wrote the song that has become the island's pop-culture anthem. "Welcome to paradise!" is now a common greeting on the two by four-mile island (where police car fenders are emblazoned with the motto *Protecting Paradise*). The words are spoken by those who live here without a hint of irony, for citizens of Key West, as well as many visitors, truly believe that this place is what Jimmy Buffet called it in another Key West–themed song, "Cheeseburger in Paradise":"heaven on earth."

Heaven on earth.
PHOTO COURTESY OF FLORIDA KEYS TDC.

BLUE CRAB CAKES
with Sweet Corn and Red Hot Aïoli

One of our day chefs, Maricia Ziegenbusch, brought this crab cake recipe with her. It's the best I've ever tasted, and it stayed with us after she left to pursue her career up north.

CRAB CAKES:

1	pound jumbo lump crabmeat, picked over
1	extra large egg, beaten slightly
2	tablespoons mayonnaise
1	teaspoon dry mustard
½	teaspoon cayenne
½	teaspoon Frank's Red Hot or Tabasco
1	teaspoon ground white pepper
3	tablespoons chopped parsley
1	cup plus 1 cup finely crushed cracker crumbs
	Vegetable oil for pan frying

SWEET CORN SALAD:

4	ears fresh sweet corn, shucked
4	scallions, white and green part, thinly sliced
1	large red tomato, peeled, seeded, and diced
2	tablespoons chopped parsley

VINAIGRETTE:

2	tablespoons cider vinegar
1	tablespoon Dijon mustard
1	tablespoon honey
1	teaspoon ground cumin seeds
2	teaspoons brown mustard seeds
6	tablespoons canola oil
	Sea salt
	Freshly ground black pepper

RED HOT AÏOLI:

1	large egg yolk
3	cloves garlic, peeled
½	teaspoon salt
2	tablespoons lemon juice
1	cup canola oil
2	tablespoons Frank's Red Hot Sauce or Tabasco

To make the crab cakes, combine the crab, egg, mayonnaise, mustard, cayenne, hot sauce, white pepper, parsley, and 1 cup of the cracker crumbs in a bowl. Mix together well. Form the mixture into 12 round cakes. Gently coat each cake with the remaining cracker crumbs. Refrigerate.

To make the corn salad, bring 2 quarts of water to a boil. Cut the kernels from the ears of corn with a sharp knife, taking care to remove any remaining bits of husk and corn silk. Cook the corn kernels in the boiling water for 4 minutes. Drain well and set aside to cool. Prepare the vinaigrette while the corn is cooling. When the corn is cool, add the scallions, tomato, and parsley. Toss the salad with the vinaigrette and refrigerate until ready to serve.

To make the vinaigrette, mix the vinegar, Dijon mustard, and honey in a small bowl with the cumin and mustard seeds. Whisk in the canola oil. Season to taste with the salt and pepper.

To make the Red Hot Aïoli, place the egg yolk, garlic, salt, and lemon juice in the work bowl of a food processor. Process to a smooth paste. With the machine running, slowly drizzle in the oil to form a thick emulsion. Add the hot sauce to taste. The aïoli should really be "zingy." Transfer the aïoli to a squeeze bottle with a medium tip, or to a small bowl. Refrigerate.

To serve, heat ½ inch of vegetable oil in a wide, deep skillet. Add the crab cakes, in batches if necessary, cook until golden brown on one side, and then carefully turn them over and cook the other side. Drain the crab cakes on paper towels. Divide the corn salad among four appetizer plates. Arrange three crab cakes over the corn on each plate. Drizzle the aïoli over the crab cakes and corn, or spoon a small dollop onto each cake.

MAKES 4 SERVINGS

CRISP FRIED MARINATED SHRIMP
with Somen Noodle Salad

Both the fried shrimp and the noodle salad are good on their own, but together they make a perfect appetizer or light lunch entrée.

SHRIMP:	
3	*garlic cloves, peeled and roughly chopped*
1	*ounce fresh ginger, peeled and roughly chopped*
1	*small yellow onion, peeled and roughly chopped*
2	*jalapeños, stemmed and seeded*
¼	*cup cilantro, chopped*
¼	*cup fresh lemon juice*
1	*teaspoon sea salt*
¼	*teaspoon fresh ground black pepper*
1	*pound jumbo Gulf shrimp (16 to 20), peeled and deveined, tails left intact*

SOMEN NOODLE SALAD:	
½	*(12-ounce) package Japanese somen noodles*
1	*tablespoon roasted sesame oil*
3	*scallions, very finely sliced*
1	*small red bell pepper, stemmed, seeded, and finely diced*
1	*small carrot, peeled and finely diced*
¼	*cup fresh cilantro, chopped*
1	*cup Ponzu (page 102)*
6	*ounces firm tofu, cut into ¼-inch cubes*
1	*egg*
1	*cup breadcrumbs*
4	*cups canola oil, for frying*
1	*tablespoon toasted sesame seeds*
1	*lime, cut into wedges for garnish*

In the jar of a blender combine the garlic, ginger, onion, jalapeños, cilantro, lemon juice, salt, and pepper. Blend to a smooth paste, adding a tablespoon or more of water if necessary for a smooth consistency. Transfer the paste to a small bowl, add the shrimp, and toss them well to coat with the marinade. Cover the bowl and refrigerate for at least 1 hour or as long as overnight.

To make the salad, cook the somen noodles according to the package directions; drain them, rinse them, and drain them again. Place the noodles in a bowl and toss

with the sesame oil. Add the scallions, bell pepper, carrot, cilantro, and the cup of Ponzu; mix well. Add the tofu and mix gently. Refrigerate the mixture. The salad can be made several hours in advance.

Beat the egg in a small bowl and place the breadcrumbs in a larger one. Lift the shrimp out of the marinade, allowing whatever clings to them to remain. Dip them first in the egg, then in the breadcrumbs, turning to coat them well. Set the shrimp aside for at least 10 minutes, or refrigerate them for up to 2 hours. When ready to cook, heat the canola oil to 360°F in a deep pan. Add the shrimp and cook them, turning occasionally, for about 4 minutes or until the breadcrumbs are golden brown and crisp. Remove the shrimp with a slotted spoon to a paper towel-lined plate. While the shrimp are cooking, divide the noodle salad among four appetizer plates, mounding it in the center. Pour any remaining Ponzu in the bowl over the noodles. Arrange the fried shrimp around the noodle salad. Sprinkle with the sesame seeds and garnish with lime wedges.

MAKES 4 SERVINGS

MUSSELS STEAMED IN COCONUT MILK
with Lemon Grass and Coriander

We nearly always have a mussel dish on the menu, usually different ones for lunch and dinner. This one has appeared sporadically since 1987 and remains a favorite.

4	*pounds fresh mussels, rinsed, cleaned of barnacles, and debearded*
1	*cup unsweetened coconut milk*
½	*cup Lemon Grass Pesto (page 105)*
1	*cup cilantro leaves, loosely packed*

Combine the mussels, coconut milk, and lemon grass pesto in a large deep pot with a tight-fitting lid. Cover the pot, place over high heat, and cook for 5 minutes, occasionally giving it a good shake, or until the mussels have opened. Divide the mussels among four bowls and ladle equal parts of the cooking liquid over them. Scatter the cilantro leaves over the mussels and serve.

MAKES 4 SERVINGS

CAVATELLI

A long-time waiter at Louie's, Donald Coladangelo, brought a plate of cavatelli he'd made at home to work with him one evening. I'd never seen it before. The next day I asked him to come to work early to show me how to make it. He brought his aunt's recipe with him and showed me the technique of rolling the little discs of dough with a fingertip to make the hollow impression on one side. This is the recipe Donald brought. He says the dough is right when it's soft like a baby's behind.

1	*cup whole milk ricotta cheese*
1	*extra large egg*
2	*tablespoons water*
2	*cups all-purpose flour (more, as necessary)*

Mix the ricotta, egg, and water in a medium bowl until well blended. Add the flour and mix with your hands to make a smooth, soft dough that is not at all sticky. Add more flour as necessary. Set the dough aside and let it rest for at least 30 minutes. Pinch off a golf-ball-sized piece of the dough. On a well-floured board with floured hands, roll the dough into a long rope about ½ inch in diameter. Repeat with the remaining dough. Working with one rope at a time, still on a floured board with floured hands, cut the dough into ½-inch segments. Press on the side of each piece with your index finger to make a hollow impression, rolling the piece against the board as you press. The cavatelli should look like little canoes. (Alternatively, use a cavatelli maker, available at specialty food equipment shops, according to the manufacturer's directions.) Spread the cavatelli on a sheet pan dusted with flour, taking care that they don't touch or they'll stick together. When all of the dough has been shaped, bring a large pot of salted water to a boil over high heat. Add the cavatelli and cook them, stirring occasionally, for 2 to 3 minutes. Remove them with a slotted spoon to a bowl of ice water. Drain them, place in a small bowl, and toss them with 1 tablespoon olive oil. Refrigerate if they won't be used right away.

MAKES 4 TO 6 SERVINGS

CAVATELLI WITH SHRIMP,
Prosciutto, Swiss Chard, and Butternut Squash

In the subtropical climate of Key West, there isn't a marked change in the seasons like there is up north. But when the first cold front reaches us in mid-October, after the dog days of August have stretched clear through September, we remember what Fall is like and turn to dishes like this one, with its earthy flavors and rich green and gold colors.

1	bunch Swiss chard
½	small butternut squash
2	tablespoons unsalted butter
1	teaspoon chopped garlic
2	ounces imported prosciutto, cut into julienne
1	pound (about 24) large gulf shrimp, peeled and deveined
1	cup cream
1	pinch of crushed red pepper flakes
	Sea salt
	Freshly ground black pepper
1	recipe Cavatelli (page 34)

Trim the stems from the Swiss chard and discard. Wash the leaves well, dry them, and cut them into a fine chiffonade. There should be about 2 cups. Peel the squash with a swivel bladed peeler, remove the seeds, and cut the squash into ¼-inch cubes. There should be a generous cup of squash. Cook the squash in an abundant quantity of boiling, salted water for 3 minutes. Drain. Melt the butter in a wide skillet over medium heat and add the chopped garlic. Let the garlic cook for a minute or so and then add the prosciutto and stir. After another minute add the shrimp, stir or toss to coat with the flavored butter, and cook for another minute. Add the squash, the Swiss chard, and the cream. Turn the heat to high and cook until the cream has reduced by one third, stirring constantly. Add the cavatelli and red pepper flakes. Continue to cook until the sauce is thick and glossy. Season with the salt and black pepper to taste. Serve hot.

MAKES 4 TO 6 SERVINGS

GRILLED GULF SHRIMP AND CHORIZO SAUSAGE
with Peppers, Onions, and Sherry Vinegar

This is one of Norman van Aken's (Louie's head chef during the seventies) original recipes for Louie's Backyard. It's still a popular item when it appears on the menu.

1½	pounds Chorizo (page 38, or use purchased sausage)

SHRIMP MARINADE:

¼	cup chopped Italian parsley
¼	cup chopped cilantro
4	cloves garlic, minced
2	tablespoons fresh lemon juice
¼	cup sherry vinegar
½	cup fresh breadcrumbs
¼	teaspoon ground mace
½	teaspoon dry oregano
2	teaspoons hot paprika
1	teaspoon sea salt
½	teaspoon fresh ground black pepper
½	cup extra virgin olive oil
2	pounds (about 36) jumbo Gulf shrimp, peeled and deveined, tail shells left intact

AÏOLI:

1	extra large egg yolk
3	cloves garlic, peeled, minced
½	teaspoon sea salt
⅛	teaspoon cayenne
1	tablespoon sherry vinegar
¾	cup extra virgin olive oil
2	tablespoons olive oil
1	red bell pepper, stemmed, seeded, and cut into 1-inch squares
1	yellow bell pepper, stemmed, seeded, and cut into 1-inch squares
1	green bell pepper, stemmed, seeded, and cut into 1-inch squares
1	large red onion, peeled and cut into 1-inch squares
2	tablespoons sherry vinegar
1	large lime, cut into wedges for garnish

For the sausage, preheat the oven to 350°F. Prick the casing several times with the tip of a knife, coil it in the bottom of a wide ovenproof skillet, and add ½ inch of water to the pan. Cook in the oven for 20 to 25 minutes, or until the meat is fully cooked, turning the sausage over halfway through the cooking time. Transfer the sausage to a plate and refrigerate it for at least one hour, preferably longer, until the meat is chilled and firm. Slice the cold, cooked chorizo into ½ -inch-thick slices. If the chorizo is purchased cooked, simply slice it as you would above.

To make the shrimp marinade, in a large bowl mix together the parsley, cilantro, garlic, lemon juice, vinegar, breadcrumbs, mace, oregano, paprika, salt, pepper, and olive oil. Toss the shrimp to coat them evenly with the marinade. Cover the bowl and refrigerate for at least 30 minutes or as long as overnight.

To make the aïoli, place the egg yolk, garlic, salt, cayenne, and sherry vinegar in the work bowl of a food processor. With the machine running, add the virgin olive oil in a small stream to form a thick emulsion. Transfer the aïoli to a plastic squeeze bottle with a medium tip or a small bowl. Refrigerate.

Heat a gas or charcoal grill to very hot. Thread the shrimp and sausage slices onto bamboo skewers. Grill over high heat for 6 to 8 minutes, until the sausages are nicely browned and sizzling and the shrimp are cooked through. While the shrimp and sausage are grilling, heat the 2 tablespoons of olive oil in a wide skillet until it is nearly smoking. Add the bell peppers and onions and sauté them over high heat until slightly softened and colored. Add the sherry vinegar to the pan, toss or stir well, and remove the pan from the heat. Divide the hot onions and peppers among 6 or 8 appetizer plates. Arrange the shrimp and sausage slices over the vegetables and drizzle with the aïoli. Garnish with the lime wedges.

MAKES 6 TO 8 SERVINGS

CHORIZO

Chorizo is a spicy pork sausage used in Spanish and Mexican cuisines. The Spanish versions are usually slightly less spicy, and smoked, while the Mexican versions, like this one, can be very fiery. Be sure not to grind the pork and fatback too fine; a coarse texture is essential to a good chorizo. Chorizo is delicious added to Paella, or used in place of Andouille sausage in gumbo.

2½	pounds boneless pork shoulder	¾	cup dry red wine
1	pound unsalted fatback	1	tablespoon garlic, minced
2	tablespoons kosher salt	1	tablespoon crushed red pepper
2	teaspoons black pepper	1	tablespoon cayenne
6	tablespoons hot paprika	3	jalapeños, stemmed, seeded, and minced
2	teaspoons ground cumin		
2	teaspoons ground coriander	2	teaspoons dry oregano
2	teaspoons sugar	1	tablespoon chili powder
			About 4 feet of hog casing

Cut the pork and fatback into 2-inch cubes; in a mixing bowl combine with the salt, black pepper, paprika, cumin, coriander, sugar wine, garlic, red pepper, cayenne, jalapeños, oregano, and chili powder. Cover the bowl and refrigerate it overnight. Grind the mixture with an electric meat grinder, using the large plate. Stuff the mixture into the hog casing, leaving it in one long piece. Refrigerate. The sausage meat can be used in some recipes without stuffing it into the casing. Simply grind the marinated meat, wrap it well, and refrigerate or freeze it.

MAKES 3½ TO 4 POUNDS SAUSAGE

Note: If you don't have the equipment for sausage-making, this can be prepared successfully by using ground pork and shaping the mixture into balls or patties instead of stuffing it into casings.

CONCH FRITTERS
with Hot Pepper Jelly and Wasabi

The queen conch, known by most people by its large, colorful pink shell, used to be so abundant in the waters around Key West that the locals became known as "Conchs." The meat of the conch is very sweet, in the way that Maine Lobster is sweet, although it tends to be tough and must be chopped, ground, or pounded before it is cooked. Fritters, where the ground conch is bound by a breading and fried, are my favorite way of enjoying conch. I make a point of eating conch fritters wherever I can find them. I've still never found a better fritter than can be made with this recipe.

1	extra large egg		2	tablespoons finely diced green bell pepper
½	cup milk		2	teaspoons minced jalapeño
1¼	cups all-purpose flour		¼	cup beer
½	teaspoon sea salt		4	squirts Tabasco
2	tablespoons baking powder		6	cups vegetable oil, for frying
1	pound conch meat, peeled, trimmed, and ground		1	cup Hot Pepper Jelly (page 104)
2	tablespoons finely chopped yellow onion		2	tablespoons wasabi powder, mixed to a stiff paste with water
2	tablespoons finely diced red bell pepper			

Beat the egg and milk together in a medium bowl. Sift in the flour, salt, and baking powder and stir well. Add the conch, onions, peppers, beer, and Tabasco and mix thoroughly. Refrigerate until ready to cook. Heat the oil in a deep pot to 360°F. Add tablespoonfuls of the fritter batter to the oil and fry for about 7 minutes or until the fritters are a deep brown and cooked through the center. Drain the fritters on paper towels. Serve with a bowl of the pepper jelly and the wasabi. The fritters are best eaten by spreading a bit of the wasabi on each, then dipping it in the pepper jelly.

MAKES 4 TO 6 SERVINGS

GRILLED PROSCIUTTO-WRAPPED SHRIMP
with Black Olive Spaetzle and Orange Aïoli

This dish is full of big Mediterranean flavors, perfect for waking up appetites on warm, sultry evenings—like most evenings in Key West. The grilled shrimp are also perfect served on their own or drizzled with the aïoli, as cocktail party fare.

2	pounds jumbo Gulf shrimp, peeled and deveined, tail shells left intact
1	tablespoon extra virgin olive oil
1	teaspoon crushed red pepper flakes
20	large, thin slices imported Prosciutto di Parma (see note)

SPAETZLE:

4	extra large egg yolks
1	cup milk
½	teaspoon sea salt
½	teaspoon ground black pepper
½	cup puréed Kalamata olives
2	cups all-purpose flour
1	tablespoon plus 2 tablespoons olive oil

AÏOLI:

1	extra large egg yolk
1	tablespoon lemon juice
1	tablespoon orange juice
1	teaspoon grated orange zest
2	cloves fresh garlic, finely chopped
½	teaspoon sea salt
1	cup extra virgin olive oil

Toss the shrimp with the olive oil and pepper flakes. Cut each slice of prosciutto in half lengthwise and use a half slice to wrap each shrimp. Thread the shrimp onto bamboo skewers and refrigerate until ready to cook.

To make the spaetzle, combine the egg yolks and milk in a mixing bowl and beat well. Add the salt, pepper, and olive purée and mix again. Stir in the flour, adding up to ½ cup additional, if necessary, to make a stiff batter that pulls away from the sides of the bowl. Bring a large pot of salted water to a boil over high heat. Position a colander or perforated pan with holes ½ inch in diameter over the boiling water and, using a rubber spatula, push the spaetzle batter through the holes into the water. Work with about a half cup of spaetzle batter at a time. When the little dumplings float to the top of the pot, remove them with a skimmer or slotted spoon and drop them in a bowl of ice water. Repeat with the remaining spaetzle batter. When all the spaetzle has been cooked, drain it, toss it with 1 tablespoon of the olive oil, and refrigerate it.

To make the aïoli, in the work bowl of a food processor combine the egg yolk, lemon and orange juices, orange zest, garlic, and sea salt. Turn on the machine and drizzle in the 1 cup olive oil to form a thick emulsion. Transfer the aïoli to a plastic squeeze bottle with a medium tip or to a small bowl and refrigerate it.

To finish and serve the dish, heat a gas or charcoal grill until very hot. Grill the shrimp skewers, turning once, for 5 minutes or until the prosciutto is browned and crisp and the shrimp are just cooked through. Remove the skewers from the grill and pull the shrimp off the skewers onto a plate. While the shrimp are grilling, heat the remaining 2 tablespoons of olive oil in a wide heavy skillet. When it is hot add the spaetzle and cook it, stirring and tossing occasionally for 5 minutes or until the spaetzle is hot and about half of it has become a toasty golden brown. Divide the spaetzle among eight appetizer plates. Arrange five shrimp over the spaetzle on each plate and drizzle the aïoli over the shrimp. Serve hot.

MAKES 8 SERVINGS

Note: You may substitute strips of blanched bacon if you can't find the Prosciutto di Parma.

Doug Shook, Chef

Doug Shook had no ambition to be a chef, and he never went to culinary school. Growing up in Virginia, he wanted to be an actor. He went to San Francisco after college and got a job, like so many actors, waiting tables at a French bistro. After six weeks, to do something different, he took a job with the chef. "Then," Doug recalls, "he suddenly quit and there I was: the only person in that kitchen who knew anything . . . and that wasn't much!" He made it work for two weeks until the restaurant was able to hire a new chef, a Frenchman who didn't like Doug. "The owners were grateful to me for staying on when the previous guy had left, so they wouldn't let the new chef fire me," remembers Doug. "He had to teach me everything, which he did reluctantly. My lack of formal education drove him crazy. Within a year, the French chef was fired, and I stayed. I had learned so much of the basics from him, and important as those basics are, I didn't exactly go by the rules. It was like being taught the proper fingering for the clarinet, but then going on to play jazz. I learned classic cooking, but I was still doing it by the seat of my pants. I still do, and hope I always will."

Doug Shook on the job in 1987.

From California he returned East and worked for a D.C. caterer who had a passion for ethnic foods. But Washington, D.C. did not suit Doug. "People were so serious there," he says. "I was the only person in town who didn't wear a tie." When Doug and his wife came to visit friends in Key West in 1985, the experience was a culture shock . . . and such a welcome one that they decided to stay. At the time, the kitchen of Louie's Backyard was being run by protean chef Norman Van Aken. He hired Doug, and when Van Aken left to open his own restaurant, Shook took over.

Doug Shook's kitchen exudes creativity. He explains, "People who have worked here a while know not to bother me when I'm standing at the door with a faraway look in my eyes and a zucchini in my hand; they know I am conjuring up a dish. It's like the whirring wheels of a slot machine. I go through all the possibilities in my head. That's the real fun of it: doing things fresh every day. Inventing is the joy of cooking.

SEARED SEA SCALLOPS
with Watercress, Miso Sauce, and Sesame Crisps

The scallops for this dish must be fresh dry-pack or "diver" scallops. Frozen scallops or those packed in water will not sear properly, but simply release their liquid and literally stew in their own juice. Black sesame seeds can be omitted if they prove hard to find, and wonton skins or egg roll wrappers can be substituted for the thin spring roll wrappers.

MISO SAUCE:

4	tablespoons rice wine vinegar
1	tablespoon soy sauce
3	tablespoons miso paste, preferably yellow
1	tablespoon grated fresh ginger
2	teaspoons sugar
1	tablespoon Chinese chile paste with garlic
1	tablespoon canola oil
1	tablespoon roasted sesame oil

SESAME CRISPS:

2	tablespoons white sesame seeds
2	tablespoons black sesame seeds
1	extra large egg white
4	sheets spring roll wrappers
2	cups canola oil (for frying)

SCALLOPS:

12	large dry-pack fresh sea scallops
1	plus 1 tablespoon canola oil
	Sea salt
	Freshly ground black pepper
1	bunch fresh watercress, large stems removed, washed, and dried

To make the miso sauce, combine the vinegar, soy sauce, miso paste, ginger, sugar, and chile paste in the work bowl of a food processor fitted with the steel blade. Process to a smooth paste. With the machine running, slowly add the canola and sesame oils as though you were making a mayonnaise. Transfer the sauce to a small bowl.

To make the sesame crisps, mix the sesame seeds together and spread them on a wide plate or cookie sheet. Whip the egg white until it is foamy. With a pastry brush, paint both sides of one of the spring roll wrappers with the egg white and press each side into the sesame seeds to form an even coating. Repeat with the remaining spring roll wrappers. Heat the canola oil in a wide skillet to 360°F. Slide in one of the wrappers and fry for about 45 seconds. Turn it over with tongs and fry the second side for about 15 seconds more, or until the wrapper is browned and crisp. Remove the wrapper from the oil and drain on paper towels. Repeat with the remaining wrappers.

For the scallops, in a small bowl toss the scallops with one tablespoon of canola oil and season them with salt and pepper. Heat the remaining canola oil in a cast iron skillet or other heavy-bottom skillet over high heat until it is very hot. Add the scallops, one at a time, leaving space between them to insure that they sear in the skillet and don't steam. Cook the scallops for about 2 minutes, until they are richly colored on one side. Carefully turn them over and sear the second side. The cooking time will depend on the size of the scallops, but 5 minutes total should be long enough for even very large ones. They should be cooked to medium rare, still translucent in the center.

While the scallops are searing, divide the watercress among four appetizer plates. Arrange three scallops on each plate. Drizzle the miso sauce over the scallops and watercress. With your fingers, break the fried sesame crisps into large, uneven shards. Tuck them into the greens. Serve at once.

MAKES 4 SERVINGS

TIMBALES OF BRIOCHE AND SMOKED TROUT
with Sour Cream and Caviar

This is really a bread pudding, rich and seductive. It makes a substantial first course or an excellent brunch entrée. Smoked salmon can be substituted for the trout, and the caviar can be omitted if desired.

1	loaf brioche (about 1 pound), or other rich egg bread	12	ounces cream cheese
6	extra large egg yolks	4	scallions, thinly sliced
2	cups cream	4	handfuls mixed baby lettuces
1	teaspoon sea salt	1	teaspoon vinegar
½	teaspoon freshly ground black pepper	1	tablespoon extra virgin olive oil
		8	tablespoons sour cream
8	ounces boneless smoked trout, picked over carefully	2	ounces caviar (Beluga is great but so is whitefish, flying fish, or trout roe)

A large muffin tin or eight 6-ounce custard cups are required to assemble this dish. Trim the ends from the brioche and cut the loaf into 16 equal slices. Using round cutters cut the slices into eight 2-inch and eight 3-inch circles. (If you are using small soufflé molds with straight sides, make all the circles the same size.) Line the cups of the muffin tin or the custard cups with plastic wrap, leaving a generous overhang. Beat the egg yolks in a mixing bowl and whisk in the cream, salt, and pepper. Add the smaller circles of brioche to the egg mixture and push them down under the surface. The brioche should become saturated with the mixture. Place one soaked brioche circle in the bottom of each cup. Divide the smoked trout among the cups. Divide the cream cheese into eight equal portions and distribute them among the cups. Do the same with the sliced scallions. Soak the larger circles of brioche in the egg mixture and place one on the top of each cup. Pour any remaining egg mixture into the cups, distributing it evenly.

Preheat the oven to 350°F. Place the muffin tin or custard cups on a sheet pan with 1-inch sides and place it on the middle shelf of the preheated oven. Pour hot water to a depth of ½ inch into the sheet pan, taking care that no water gets into the cups. Bake for 30 minutes until the tops of the timbales are lightly browned and the custard is set.

Remove from the oven and allow to cool. When cool enough to handle, remove the timbales from the plastic-lined cups and invert them onto a dry sheet pan. Increase the oven heat to 400°F.

To serve the timbales, return them to the oven and bake them for 10 to 12 minutes or until they are hot in the center and lightly browned all around. Toss the baby lettuces with the vinegar and oil and arrange the lettuce in the center of eight small plates. Carefully place a timbale on top of the greens. Add a generous tablespoon of sour cream to the top of each timbale and spoon the caviar onto the sour cream. Serve right away.

MAKES 8 SERVINGS

MUSSELS STEAMED IN WHITE WINE
with Saffron, Tomatoes, and Israeli Couscous

The Israeli couscous in this dish looks like pearls and adds an interesting texture to the mussel broth. Acini di Pepi pasta, or another very small soup pasta, could be substituted for the couscous.

4	*dozen mussels, cleaned and debearded*
1	*cup dry white wine*
1	*large, red ripe tomato, peeled, seeded, and diced*
½	*cup Israeli couscous*
8	*tablespoons Saffron-Pernod Butter (page 109)*

Combine the mussels, wine, tomato, couscous, and Saffron-Pernod butter in a deep pot with a tight-fitting lid and cook, covered, until the mussels have opened. Divide the mussels among four wide soup plates, swirl the liquid and couscous around in the pot, and pour it over the mussels. Serve hot.

MAKES 4 SERVINGS

CHICKEN SATÉ
with Cashew Sauce and Mango Slaw

A saté consists of small pieces of meat, chicken, or seafood threaded onto wooden skewers and grilled. The meat is always marinated and usually served with a peanut sauce. Peeled shrimp or boneless pork would also be good cooked this way. The cilantro must be fresh. Dried cilantro has none of the flavor of fresh.

1	*pound boneless, skinless chicken breast*
3	*tablespoons canola oil*
3	*tablespoons chopped cilantro*
2	*tablespoons fresh lime juice*
2	*tablespoons soy sauce*
2	*tablespoons fresh ginger, peeled and chopped*
6	*cloves garlic, peeled and chopped*
1	*tablespoon brown sugar*
2	*teaspoons ground cumin*
½	*teaspoon crushed red pepper flakes*
2	*cups Mango Slaw (page 49)*
½	*cup Spicy Cashew Sauce (page 103)*

Cut the chicken breast lengthwise into ¾-inch-wide strips. In a small bowl, combine the canola oil, cilantro, lime juice, soy sauce, ginger, garlic, brown sugar, cumin, and red pepper flakes. Add the chicken strips and toss to coat them well. Cover the bowl and refrigerate for at least 1 hour or as long as overnight.

When ready to cook, heat a gas or charcoal grill to very hot. While the grill is heating, thread the strips of chicken onto soaked bamboo skewers. Grill the chicken skewers, turning to brown them evenly for 5 to 7 minutes, or until the chicken is cooked through. Divide the Mango Slaw among individual serving plates. Place the grilled chicken skewers on the slaw and drizzle with the Cashew Sauce.

MAKES 4 TO 6 SERVINGS

MANGO SLAW

This is a light, refreshing salad, only a little bit sweet. Jicama is a root vegetable that looks like a large brown radish with crisp white flesh and an elusive flavor. Julienned apples would make a reasonable substitute.

2	*large, slightly under-ripe mangoes*
1	*small jicama*
1	*red bell pepper*
1	*poblano pepper*
2	*jalapeños*
½	*cup chopped fresh cilantro*
2	*teaspoons ground toasted cumin seed*
½	*teaspoon freshly ground black pepper*
½	*cup freshly squeezed lime juice*

Peel and julienne the mangoes. Peel the jicama and cut it into strips the same size as the mango strips. Remove the stems and seeds from the red bell, poblano, and jalapeños and cut them julienne. Combine the peppers with the mangoes, jicama, cilantro, cumin, black pepper, and lime juice in a large bowl and toss to mix well. Refrigerate the mixture until thoroughly chilled.

MAKES ABOUT 6 CUPS

SPIEDINI OF BEEF
with Fresh Mozzarella, Tomatoes, and Pasta Pearls

I had nightmares about putting meatballs on the menu the day before this dish appeared, but it turned out to be one of the best-selling appetizers that season. And, yes, the meatballs, cheese, and pomodoro sauce make a great sandwich.

MEATBALLS:

1	pound lean ground beef
1	extra large egg
½	cup grated Pecorino Romano (see note)
½	cup dry breadcrumbs
2	tablespoons chopped Italian parsley
2	teaspoons chopped garlic
1	teaspoon sea salt
½	teaspoon freshly ground black pepper

MOZZARELLA:

1	extra large egg
1	cup flour
1½	cups dry breadcrumbs
1	tablespoon crushed red pepper flakes
1	pound fresh mozzarella, cut into 18 cubes
6	cups water, salted
1	cup Israeli couscous (see note)
1½	cups Pomodoro Sauce (page 107)
6	tablespoons olive oil
6	sprigs fresh basil

To make the meatballs, combine the ground beef, egg, Romano cheese, breadcrumbs, Italian parsley, garlic, salt, and pepper in a bowl and mix them together well with your hands. Form the mixture into 24 balls and set them aside on a plate.

For the mozzarella, beat the egg in a small bowl. Pour the flour onto a plate. On a separate plate mix together the breadcrumbs and crushed red pepper. Dip each mozzarella cube first in the flour, then the egg, and finally the crumb mixture. Set the breaded mozzarella aside on a plate.

To serve, bring salted water to a boil, add the couscous, and cook it for about 9 minutes, or until it is al dente. Drain, rinse under running water, and drain again. Heat the Pomodoro Sauce in a small pan and add the couscous. Keep warm. Thread the meatballs and breaded mozzarella onto 6 soaked bamboo skewers, alternating meatballs and cheese. Heat a gas or charcoal grill to medium hot. Brush the skewers with the olive oil and grill them, turning occasionally and basting with the oil, for 10 to 12 minutes, or until the coating on the cheese has browned nicely and the meatballs are cooked through. Divide the couscous and Pomodoro sauce among six appetizer plates, place a skewer on each, and garnish with a sprig of basil.

MAKES 6 SERVINGS

Note: Instead of the Pecorino Romano chesse you may substitute Parmesan or another pecorino, such as Sardo, Siciliano, or Toxcano.

Note: You may substitute Acini di Pepi pasta or another small soup pasta, such as orzo, for the Israeli couscous.

Big Names on Key West

Key West has attracted more than its share of famous names. These are some of the celebrities who have a special association with the island:

JOHN JAMES AUDUBON

He visited Key West in 1832 while hunting birds to draw for *Birds of America*. In fact, he never lived here, but Key West's Audubon House (which was actually the home of John H. Geiger, a sea captain who was himself a bird watcher) contains much bird art and a portrait of Lucy Audubon, John James's wife, who is reputed to have said, "I have a rival in every bird."

JOHN DOS PASSOS

The social activist writer and novelist was introduced to his wife, Kathy, by Ernest Hemingway at Hemingway's home. John and Kathy lived for a while at 1401 Pine Street in Key West.

© SCRIPPS HOWARD NEWS SERVICE

TENNESSEE WILLIAMS

He was born in Mississippi and had a home in Key West starting in the mid-1940s. He was supposedly terrified of meeting Hemingway because of Papa's famous homophobia. "Hemingway usually kicks people like me in the crotch," Williams said. The one time they met (in Cuba, not Key West), they are said to have gotten on famously because they both had alcohol-ravaged livers about which they could commiserate.

TOM MCGUANE

He is perhaps better known around his home town for being a close friend of Jimmy Buffett's than for such celebrated novels as *The Bushwhacked Piano* and *Ninety-Two in the Shade*, both of which are set in Key West (the latter filmed here).

ERNEST HEMINGWAY

He arrived in Key West from Paris in 1928 at the age of twenty-nine. Here he wrote *A Farewell to Arms* and subsequent masterworks. He hung out at Sloppy Joe's Bar (now located on Duval Street); he boxed and coached his prize roosters in cockfights at the place that is now the restaurant Blue Heaven; and he was known for owning six-toed cats, the descendants of which you will meet if you tour his home at 907 Whitehead.

Hemingway's house and one of the six-toed cats.
PHOTO COURTESY OF FLORIDA KEYS TDC.

WALLACE STEVENS

He wintered in Key West throughout the 1930s. He hung out with fellow poet Robert Frost (also a resident), but is said to have hated Hemingway and Dos Passos. Stevens won the Pulitzer Prize in 1955.

JIMMY BUFFETT

He came to Key West in the early 1970s as a not-too-successful songwriter. He loved the freewheeling attitudes of those days; and in life among the island's dopers, swashbucklers, hippies, and barflies, he found his artistic voice. At the age of twenty-six, in 1973, he recorded *A White Sport Coat and a Pink Crustacean*, which made him a star. For much of the 1970s Jimmy lived next to Louie's Backyard at 704 Waddell Street, where he sat on a porch swing and strummed his six-string. Buffett often played for meals at Louie's. In 1985 he opened Margaritaville, a vast bar and souvenir shop on Duval Street.

DIVINE

He arrived in Key West in the early 1980s and made himself at home. His wide acceptance as the island's best-known celebrity drag queen was a clear signal that alternate sexuality had become a significant part of island culture.

FRIED FRESH CALAMARI
with Romesco Sauce

Rice flour gives this fried calamari its crunch, but all-purpose flour is an acceptable substitute. The most important thing is to have fresh squid.

2	cups rice flour
1	teaspoon sea salt
1	teaspoon black pepper
½	teaspoon cayenne
1	pound fresh small calamari, skinned, cleaned, body sacs cut into ½-inch rings
6	cups vegetable oil (for frying)
1	cup Romesco Sauce (page 99)
1	lemon, cut into wedges for garnish

In a medium-sized bowl, combine the rice flour, salt, pepper, and cayenne. Mix well.

Heat the vegetable oil to 375°F in a deep pot or Dutch oven. Have ready a paper towel-lined plate, for draining the calamari, and a platter or four appetizer plates for serving. Place a bowl of Romesco Sauce in the center of the platter or small individual bowls on the plates. Add half of the calamari to the rice flour and toss to coat well. Transfer the coated calamari to a sieve and shake to remove the excess flour. Reserve the remaining rice flour. In a large skillet heat the vegetable oil on medium-high and carefully place the calamari rings and tentacles into the hot oil. Fry the calamari, moving the pieces about in the oil with a spider or slotted spoon so they don't stick together; cook for 3 minutes or until the rice flour coating is browned and crisp. Remove the calamari from the oil with the spider and place on the paper towel-lined plate to drain. Repeat with the remaining calamari. Pile the fried rings and tentacles around the bowls of Romesco Sauce on the platter or each of the smaller plates. Garnish with the lemon wedges.

MAKES 4 SERVINGS

LITTLENECK CLAMS STEAMED
with Potato Ribbons, Diced Tomato, and Herbs

Clams come in all sizes, from tiny Italian pasta clams, to big chowder clams, or quahogs, and even giant Pacific clams called geoducks, which can weigh as much as three pounds each. Littleneck clams are small hardshell clams, about the size of a silver dollar, and are very sweet and tender. They're excellent eaten raw, on the half shell, or cooked very briefly. This is a little like Linguine with Clam Sauce, with the julienned potatoes standing in for the pasta.

2	Idaho potatoes, peeled (about 1 pound)	1	tablespoon fresh thyme leaves
4	tablespoons olive oil	2	tablespoons chopped Italian parsley
8	cloves garlic, peeled and finely chopped	¼	teaspoon crushed red pepper flakes
2	tablespoons fresh lemon juice	48	littleneck clams, scrubbed well
1	cup dry white wine	1	fresh lemon, cut into wedges
1	medium red ripe tomato, peeled, seeded, and chopped (about 1 cup)		

Cut the potatoes with a mandoline into long julienne about ⅛ inch thick, or use a spiral cutter to cut the potatoes into long, curling ribbons. Drop the potatoes into a bowl of water as they are cut. Bring 2 quarts of salted water to a boil over high heat, add the drained potatoes, and cook them for 4 minutes or until the potatoes are just barely tender. The potatoes will cook further with the clams so it is important not to overcook them at this point. Remove ½ cup of the cooking water and set it aside. Drain the potatoes well and rinse them under cold water to stop the cooking. Drain again.

In a large deep pot with a tight-fitting lid, heat the olive oil. Add the chopped garlic and cook, stirring, until the garlic has colored to a pale gold and is very fragrant. Add the lemon juice and reduce it by half. Add the wine, tomatoes, potatoes, thyme, parsley, and pepper flakes. Stir well. Add the clams and the ½ cup potato cooking water, cover the pot, and cook over medium high heat for 7 to 10 minutes until the clams have opened. Divide the contents of the pot among four wide soup plates. Garnish with lemon wedges.

MAKES 4 SERVINGS

CITRUS-CURED RAINBOW TROUT

The Top of the Mountain Trout Company, which supplies us with our smoked trout, also sends us fresh "trophy trout"—beautiful six or seven pounders that look so much like salmon when they're filleted that we were inspired to treat them as such and developed this gravlax-style recipe for them. The results were delicious, yielding nearly transparent, orange slices of clean, bright-tasting fish.

1	orange
1	lemon
1	lime
½	cup kosher salt
1½	cups sugar
1	teaspoon ground white pepper
2	(3-pound) rainbow trout, filleted, pinbones removed, and skin left on

Cut the zest from the orange, lemon, and lime with a swivel bladed peeler. Combine it with the salt, sugar, and pepper in the work bowl of a food processor and process until finely chopped. Spread half of the seasoning mixture over the bottom of a glass dish large enough to hold the trout fillets in one layer. Lay the trout, skin side down, over the seasoning mixture. Squeeze the orange, lemon, and lime over the trout fillets then cover them with the remaining seasoning mixture. Cover the dish with plastic wrap and refrigerate for 24 hours. When ready to cook the trout, remove the fillets from the dish and rinse them under running water. Pat them dry with paper towels. Slice the filets on a bias as thinly as possible.

MAKES 8 SERVINGS

SALADS & DRESSINGS

Arugula Salad

Boston Lettuce and Watercress

Spiced Pecans

Hot Fried Chicken Salad

Hearts of Romaine

Salad of Melon, Grape Tomatoes, and Watercress

Smoky Chile Caesar Salad

Tomato Salad

Keith Anderson's Cole Slaw Dressing

Caesar Dressing

Smoky Chile Caesar

Creamy Lemon Vinaigrette

Creamy Apple Cider Vinaigrette

Honey Mustard Dressing

Thousand Island Dressing

Roquefort Dressing

ARUGULA SALAD
with Quince Paste and Manchego

Manchego topped with quince paste is a staple in Spanish tapas bars. Guava paste, which may be easier to find, makes a good substitute.

4	*ounces quince paste (see note) cut into 20 diamond-shaped slices*
6	*cups arugula, stems removed, washed, and dried*
6	*ounces Creamy Lemon Vinaigrette (page 70)*
1	*(4-ounce) wedge manchego cheese (see note)*

Arrange the slices of quince paste around the edges of four salad plates. Toss the arugula with the vinaigrette and mound it in the center of the plates. Shave the manchego over the salad with a swivel-blade vegetable peeler.

MAKES 4 SERVINGS

Note: Quince paste, also called Membrillo, is a Spanish specialty made of quinces that are cooked down to a firm, jelly-like paste. Guava paste, made the same way, is more readily available. If you can't find either one, small pieces of fresh, ripe cataloupe would provide the right touch of sweetness to balance the saltiness of the cheese.

Note: Instead of manchego cheese, you may use Parmesan or another pecorino, such as Sardo, Siciliano, or Toxcano.

BOSTON LETTUCE AND WATERCRESS
with Maytag Blue Cheese, Apples, and Spiced Pecans

This salad was devised as a way to feature Maytag Blue Cheese when we first discovered how creamy and delicious it is. Made in Iowa by the same family that makes the washing machines, Maytag Blue is considered one of the great blue cheeses of the world, along with Stilton, Roquefort, and Gorgonzola. This salad has been one of the most popular items on our menu since it first appeared there in 1988.

2	*heads Boston lettuce, separated into leaves, washed, and dried*
1	*bunch watercress, tough stems removed, washed, and dried*
1	*cup Creamy Apple Cider Vinaigrette (page 71)*
1	*Granny Smith apple, quartered, cored, and thinly sliced*
8	*ounces Maytag blue cheese (or any blue-veined cheese), crumbled*
1	*cup Spiced Pecans (page 61)*

Combine the Boston lettuce and watercress in a large bowl with the vinaigrette and toss very gently to coat evenly all the greens with dressing. Arrange the lettuce and watercress on four individual salad plates. Divide the apple slices among the salads, slipping them in randomly among the lettuce leaves. Crumble the blue cheese over the greens and scatter the pecans around on the salads last. Or leave the dressed greens in the salad bowl and add the garnishes before bringing the salad to the table. Serve with additional apple cider vinaigrette.

MAKES 4 SERVINGS

SPICED PECANS

These have been on the menu for nearly as long as I can remember, but we still have to store them out of sight, out of reach or under guard to keep them from mysteriously disappearing. They're an essential part of the Boston Lettuce Salad with Maytag Blue Cheese, and make an irresistible snack on their own. Other nuts, such as walnuts and macadamia nuts can be prepared the same way.

3	*quarts water*
2	*pounds jumbo pecan halves*
8	*cups peanut oil, for frying*
1	*cup confectioners' sugar*
	Sea salt
	Cayenne pepper

Bring the water to a boil in a large pot, add the pecan halves, and boil them for 5 minutes. Drain them well. Heat the peanut oil in a large, deep pot to 360°F. When the oil is hot, toss the pecans with the sugar in a large bowl to coat them well. Carefully add the pecans to the hot oil and fry, stirring occasionally, for 12 minutes or until the oil nearly stops bubbling and the pecans are a rich mahogany brown and seem "light" for their size. Drain the pecans on a parchment-lined pan and allow to cool. When the pecans are cool, season them with sea salt to taste and a liberal sprinkling of the cayenne pepper. Store in a sealed container at room temperature.

MAKES 32 1-OUNCE SERVINGS

HOT FRIED CHICKEN SALAD

Louie's former chef Norman van Aken put this salad on the lunch menu in 1985. It still outsells any entrée salad we offer.

MARINADE:

2	*jalapeños, stemmed, seeded, and thinly sliced*
1	*teaspoon hot paprika*
1	*teaspoon crushed red pepper*
1	*teaspoon freshly ground black pepper*
1	*teaspoon cayenne*
2	*cups cream or half-and-half*
6	*extra large eggs, lightly beaten*
2	*(1-pound) whole, boneless chicken breasts, skin removed*

PICKLED RED ONION:

1	*small red onion, peeled and sliced into ¼-inch rings*
1	*teaspoon sugar*
2	*teaspoons malt vinegar*
4	*cups canola oil, for frying*
1½	*cups all-purpose flour*
1	*teaspoon sea salt*
2	*teaspoons freshly ground black pepper*
2	*teaspoons crushed red pepper*
2	*romaine hearts, torn into bite-sized pieces, washed, and dried*
1	*cup Honey Mustard Dressing (page 71) or more*

For the marinade, combine the jalapeños, paprika, red pepper, black pepper, cayenne, cream, and eggs and mix well. Cut the chicken into 1-inch-wide strips and add them to the marinade. Cover and refrigerate for at least 2 hours or as long as 24.

Make the pickled onions by tossing the onion rings with the sugar and vinegar. Set aside at room temperature for 30 minutes.

To complete the salad, heat the canola oil to 375°F in a wide, deep pot or deep-fat fryer. Mix together the flour, salt, black pepper, and red pepper. Lift the chicken pieces from the marinade and dredge them with the seasoned flour. Shake off the excess and fry the chicken strips for about 5 minutes or until they are browned and crisp and cooked through. Drain the chicken strips on paper towels. Toss the torn romaine with the honey mustard dressing in a large bowl and then mound it on four deep plates or wide bowls. Cut the chicken into bite-sized pieces and divide them among the four plates. Drizzle additional dressing over the salads, if desired, and top with a few rings of pickled onion.

MAKES 4 SERVINGS

HEARTS OF ROMAINE
with Roquefort, Red Onion, and Farm Mushrooms

Blue cheese and fresh raw mushrooms complement each other well. It is important, though, that the mushrooms are snow white and crisp.

3	*romaine hearts, tops trimmed, cut into quarters lengthwise, washed, and dried*
1½	*cups Roquefort dressing (page 73)*
12	*large, unblemished , tightly closed farm mushrooms*
1	*small red onion, peeled and sliced into ¼-inch rings*

Arrange the romaine heart quarters, one lying atop a second, crosswise on six salad plates. Spoon 4 tablespoons of the dressing over each. Wipe the mushrooms clean and slice them very thinly. Scatter them over the dressing, add several rings of red onion, and serve.

MAKES 6 SERVINGS

SALAD OF MELON, GRAPE TOMATOES, AND WATERCRESS
with Basil, Prosciutto, and Chèvre

Sous-Chef Tim Lyons has a natural gift for combining just the right flavors, as this unusual salad demonstrates.

2	cups balsamic vinegar
½	honeydew melon, chilled
¼	small seedless watermelon, chilled
2	bunches watercress, tough stems removed, washed, and dried
1	teaspoon extra virgin olive oil
1	cup grape or cherry tomatoes, cut in half
8	ounces fresh goat cheese, cut into 32 pieces
24	large, unblemished, fresh basil leaves, cut into fine julienne
4	ounces prosciutto, cut in a fine julienne

Make a balsamic vinegar glaze by putting the vinegar in a small saucepan over very low heat. A flame tamer would be helpful. The vinegar should never boil, or go beyond the laziest possible simmer. Cook the vinegar until it has reduced to a syrupy consistency, about 45 to 60 minutes.

Cut the rind from the melons and cut the flesh into 2-inch wedges. Keep the melons cold. Toss the watercress with the olive oil and divide it among eight chilled salad plates. Arrange the melon pieces around the cress with the grape tomatoes. Nestle the pieces of goat cheese in among the greens. Drizzle the balsamic vinegar glaze over the fruit and the cress. Scatter the basil and prosciutto over the melon.

MAKES 8 SERVINGS

A Nice Kitchen

Kitchens of great restaurants, no matter how capacious, are almost always too small to contain the egos of the chefs that work in them. Louie's is different. Frantic though it may get at the height of dinner hour, there's a peculiar calm about the place that is unlike any important kitchen we have ever seen. To explain it, Doug Shook points from the deck out towards the clear waters of the ocean and says, "When you look out there, all the tension just washes away."

One of the most unusual things about this restaurant is the long tenures of so many of the staff, both in the kitchen and on the floor, some of whom have been here twenty-plus years, as has Doug himself. "The people who work at Louie's know that I'm not going anywhere," Doug says. "I don't have that burning ambition to move on. I like my lifestyle right here."

Without the typical jockeying for power in the kitchen, Louie's is an inspiring place to cook. Virtually every member of the staff likes to point out how stress-free it is, and how conducive to creative cooking. "Of the fifteen people working for me, thirteen have gone elsewhere, just to test the waters, and all have come back," Doug notes. "They get spoiled here. This is an unregimented kind of place. I need people who can regiment themselves; I want a kitchen that is a pleasant place to work, a nice place to spend some time."

SMOKY CHILE CAESAR SALAD
with Tortilla "Rajas"

While the original Caesar salad originated in Mexico, this one, which substitutes smoked jalapeños for anchovies, has a real south-of-the-border flavor.

3	*romaine hearts, torn into bite-sized pieces, washed, and dried*
1½	*cups Smoky Chile Caesar Dressing (page 70)*
4	*(6-inch) corn tortillas*
	Canola oil for frying
1	*teaspoon sea salt*
¼	*teaspoon cayenne*
1	*teaspoon freshly ground cumin seed*
3	*ounces grated manchego cheese*

Prepare the lettuces and salad dressing first. Keep them cold. Cut the corn tortillas into thin strips. Heat ½ inch of canola oil in a wide skillet and fry the tortilla strips, in batches, until they are browned and crisp. Drain the tortillas on paper towels. Mix the salt, cayenne, and cumin together and season the fried tortilla strips to taste with the mixture. Toss the torn romaine with the dressing to coat the leaves well. Divide the lettuce among six deep plates or salad bowls. Sprinkle the manchego over the salads and top with the warm tortilla strips.

MAKES 6 SERVINGS

TOMATO SALAD
with Herbed Chevre and Sweet Red Wine Vinaigrette

Old-fashioned "heirloom" varieties of tomatoes are being grown around the country now, and people are rediscovering how remarkable tomatoes can be. Some of the varieties of tomatoes appearing in markets now are Purple Cherokee, Green Zebra, Elberta Peach, and Red Grape. This salad takes advantage of a windfall of beautiful tomatoes.

6	*ounces fresh white goat cheese*
1	*clove garlic, peeled and finely chopped*
2	*teaspoons fresh thyme leaves*
1	*teaspoon freshly ground black pepper*
4	*teaspoons red wine vinegar*
1	*large shallot, peeled and finely chopped*
½	*teaspoon sea salt*
1	*teaspoon sugar*
¾	*cup extra virgin olive oil*
4	*to 6 heirloom tomatoes, preferably several varieties*
6	*oil-cured black olives, slivered*
12	*large, unblemished basil leaves, cut into thin strips*
1	*Vidalia onion, peeled and cut into ¼-inch rings*

Blend the goat cheese, garlic, thyme, and pepper with a fork in a small bowl. Divide into six equal portions and shape the cheese mixture into balls or ovals. Whisk together the vinegar, shallot, salt, and sugar. Whisk in the olive oil. Taste the vinaigrette. If it seems very sharp, dilute it with a tablespoon or so of water. Remove the cores from the tomatoes and cut them into wedges. Arrange them casually in the bottom of six wide soup bowls. Place a portion of the goat cheese in the center of each. Ladle the vinaigrette evenly over the tomatoes. Scatter the olives, basil, and onion rings over the tomatoes and serve with crusty bread.

MAKES 6 SERVINGS

KEITH ANDERSON'S BETTER-THAN-EXCELLENT COLESLAW DRESSING

Keith was the day chef at Louie's in 1989 and 1990. When he was developing his lunch menu he was very concerned with having a coleslaw for the sandwich plates that people would remember and tried dozens of recipes in search of one. This is the one that came out on top and the one we still use today.

3	cloves fresh garlic, chopped
6	tablespoons champagne vinegar
1	tablespoon cornstarch
1	cup cream
3	extra large eggs
3	tablespoons sugar
1	tablespoon honey
2½	teaspoons dry mustard
1½	teaspoons celery seed
½	teaspoon sea salt
½	teaspoon freshly ground black pepper
¼	teaspoon cayenne
2	cups mayonnaise

In a medium mixing bowl combine the garlic, vinegar, cornstarch, cream, eggs, sugar, honey, mustard, celery seed, sea salt, black pepper, and cayenne and mix until smooth with a wire whisk. Place the bowl over a pot of simmering water and cook it, stirring occasionally with the whisk, until it has thickened enough to allow a glimpse of the bowl's bottom when it is stirred. Remove the bowl from the heat and set it aside to cool at least 20 minutes. Whisk in the mayonnaise. Store the dressing in the refrigerator.

MAKES ABOUT 4 CUPS

CAESAR DRESSING

The success of this dressing depends on good vinegar, good oil, and good cheese. We use a French red wine vinegar, aged in oak barrels, a bright green Spanish extra virgin olive oil, and freshly grated Parmigiano Reggiano. Seek out a vinegar that has a true wine flavor, an extra virgin olive oil that is fruity and silky, and invest in a piece of real Italian Parmigiano; it will keep for weeks in the refrigerator.

2	extra large egg yolks	2	teaspoons fresh garlic, chopped
¼	cup sherry vinegar	2	teaspoons freshly ground black pepper
3	tablespoons lemon juice		
2	teaspoons Dijon mustard	1	cup extra virgin olive oil
2	chipotle chiles packed in adobo, drained	½	cup grated Manchego cheese (or more)

In the work bowl of a food processor, combine the egg yolks with the vinegar, lemon juice, mustard, chiles, garlic, and pepper. Process to combine well. With the machine running, drizzle in the oil to make a thick emulsion. Add the cheese and process for a few seconds longer. Put in a glass container and store in the refrigerator.

MAKES ABOUT 2½ CUPS

SMOKY CHILE CAESAR

Chipotle chiles are dried, smoked jalapeños. They can be bought in cans, packed in adobo sauce, or dried. If dried chiles are used, they should be soaked in warm water for thirty minutes to soften them, and the stems and seeds should be removed.

2	*extra large egg yolks*	2	*teaspoons fresh garlic, chopped*
¼	*cup red wine vinegar*	2	*teaspoons freshly ground black pepper*
3	*tablespoons lemon juice*		
2	*teaspoons Dijon mustard*	1	*cup extra virgin olive oil*
2	*chipotle chiles packed in adobo, drained*	½	*cup grated Parmesan cheese (or more)*

Combine the egg yolks, vinegar, lemon juice, mustard, chiles, garlic, and black pepper in the work bowl of a food processor and process to a smooth paste. With the machine running, slowly add the oil. When all of the oil has been incorporated, add the cheese and process for a few seconds longer. Put in a glass container and store in the refrigerator.

MAKES 2 TO 3 CUPS

CREAMY LEMON VINAIGRETTE

This is another light dressing, good for soft lettuces. It's also good drizzled over lightly fried fish fillets.

2	*extra large egg yolks*	¾	*teaspoon sea salt*
2	*teaspoons grated lemon zest*	1¼	*cups extra virgin olive oil*
4	*tablespoons fresh lemon juice*	½	*cup cream*

Whisk together the egg yolks, lemon zest, lemon juice, and salt in a small mixing bowl. Gradually whisk in the oil and cream. Put in a glass container and store in the refrigerator.

MAKES ABOUT 2 ½ CUPS

CREAMY APPLE CIDER VINAIGRETTE

The sour cream in this recipe takes the place of egg yolks to give the dressing a smooth, homogeneous texture. Be sure to use a real apple cider vinegar, not just flavored white vinegar. Organic cider vinegar is best.

1	*cup cider vinegar*	2	*teaspoons Dijon mustard*
2	*cups canola oil*	2	*teaspoons freshly ground black pepper*
¼	*cup sour cream*	1	*cup clover honey*

Combine the vinegar, oil, sour cream, mustard, pepper, and honey in the jar of a blender and blend for 1 minute. Store in the refrigerator.

MAKES ABOUT 3½ CUPS

HONEY MUSTARD DRESSING

This is a great salad dressing, whether it's served with the Hot Fried Chicken Salad or just torn crisp greens.

3	*extra large egg yolks*	1½	*cups canola oil*
2	*teaspoons honey*	½	*cup olive oil*
6	*teaspoons Creole mustard*	2	*teaspoons roasted sesame oil*
½	*cup balsamic vinegar*		

Combine the egg yolks with the honey, mustard, and vinegar in a mixing bowl. Whisking constantly, slowly drizzle in the canola, olive, and sesame oils to make a smooth emulsion. Keep the dressing cold.

MAKES ABOUT 3 CUPS

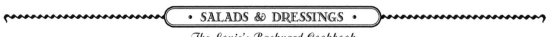
THOUSAND ISLAND DRESSING

This creamy dressing is often disregarded as old-fashioned or unsophisticated, but when made with fresh home-made mayonnaise it's lifted above the ordinary. Try it with chilled shrimp over a bed of soft lettuces with wedges of tomato.

3	*extra large egg yolks*
2	*tablespoons lemon juice*
½	*teaspoon sea salt*
¼	*teaspoon freshly ground black pepper*
¼	*teaspoon cayenne*
2	*cups olive oil*
1	*cup canola oil*
¾	*cup chile sauce*
6	*tablespoons sweet pickle relish*
4	*scallions, thinly sliced*
4	*hard-cooked eggs, peeled and chopped*

Make a mayonnaise first by combining the egg yolks, lemon juice, sea salt, black pepper, and cayenne in the work bowl of a food processor. With the machine running, slowly add the olive and canola oils to form a thick emulsion. Transfer the mayonnaise to a mixing bowl and stir in the chile sauce, pickle relish, scallions, and cooked eggs. Put in a glass container and store the dressing in the refrigerator.

MAKES ABOUT 5 CUPS

ROQUEFORT DRESSING

Another blue cheese can be substituted for the Roquefort, but it should be a good one, such as Maytag or Great Hill Blue. Obviously, this is also a great dip for raw vegetables.

½	cup finely diced yellow onion
1½	teaspoons fresh garlic, chopped
2	teaspoons lemon juice
8	anchovy fillets, drained, chopped
½	cup champagne vinegar
½	pound Roquefort cheese, crumbled
1½	cups sour cream
½	cup cream
½	cup canola oil
½	cup olive oil
½	cup grated Parmesan cheese
1	teaspoon dried marjoram
1	tablespoon chopped Italian parsley
2	scallions, thinly sliced

This dressing is best made in an electric mixer with a paddle attachment, or mixed by hand with a wooden spoon. A food processor will make it too homogenous. Combine the onion, garlic, lemon juice, anchovies, vinegar, and Roquefort cheese. Mix with the paddle or wooden spoon until well combined. Slowly add the sour cream, cream, canola and olive oils. Stir in the Parmesan cheese, marjoram, parsley, and scallions. Put in a glass container and store in the refrigerator.

MAKES 1½ QUARTS

Darlene Ciulla, Pantry Chef

Darlene Ciulla is one of the reasons each plate of food sent forth from Louie's kitchen is good-looking. "Presentation is so important," she observes. "So is speed. I get to know the recipes; I watch over salads, appetizers, and desserts; I make the dressings; I don't make the desserts, but I garnish them."

Darlene learned to cook in Boston, working at the celebrated Harvest restaurant, where she says she learned about fine dining. Since first visiting Key West she knew that Louie's Backyard would be a great place to work; and she now describes Doug Shook as a kind of culinary mentor. "He treats his people with respect," she says. "In return, he gets dedication and loyalty. We become like a family; and although I leave every once in a while, I always come back."

She says that having a job in this place is immensely rewarding, but can also be very difficult on an island known for its casual libertinism. The recipes are intricate, the small kitchen must operate at utmost efficiency. There is no room for sloven work. "You need to show up sober," she says. "And for many in Key West, that isn't necessarily always the case."

SOUPS

Dark Beer and English Cheddar Soup

Asparagus and Mushroom Velouté

Bahamian Conch Chowder

Chilled Buttermilk Soup

Black Bean Purée

Chilled Celery Root Soup

Creamy Leek Soup

Yellow Pepper Soup

Shellfish and Hot Sausage Gumbo

Tomatillo and Avocado Soup

Chilled Carrot Soup

Cuban Style White Bean Soup

Gazpacho

DARK BEER AND ENGLISH CHEDDAR SOUP
with Rye Croutons

When this appears on a New Year's Day brunch menu, it's called "Hair of the Dog Soup."

6	tablespoons butter
3	medium yellow onions, peeled, sliced thin
6	garlic cloves, peeled and minced
6	tablespoons all-purpose flour
2	(12-ounce) bottles premium dark beer
2	cups chicken stock or canned chicken broth
2	medium boiling potatoes, peeled and cut up
1	bay leaf
1	sprig fresh thyme
1	pound aged English Cheddar, the sharper the better, grated
1	cup heavy cream or half-and-half
2	teaspoons salt
½	teaspoon cayenne pepper

Melt the butter over medium-high heat in a large soup pot or Dutch oven. When the foam subsides, add the onions. Cook the onions, stirring often, until they are softened and beginning to turn straw-colored. Stir in the garlic and cook 5 minutes longer, taking care that the garlic doesn't color at all. Stir in the flour and cook for 5 minutes longer. Stir in the beer, chicken stock, and potatoes. Add the bay leaf and fresh thyme. Bring the liquid to a simmer and cook for 20 minutes, or until the potatoes are very tender. Remove the pot from the heat and stir in the grated Cheddar. Purée the soup, either with an immersion blender or in small batches in a regular blender. Strain the soup through a medium-mesh sieve, rinse out the pot, and return the soup to the pot. Stir in the cream and season with the salt and cayenne pepper. Reheat the soup over medium heat, stirring well and taking care not to let it boil. Serve the soup in wide, rimmed soup bowls garnished with Rye Croutons (page 105).

MAKES 8 SERVINGS (2 QUARTS)

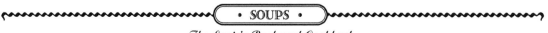

ASPARAGUS AND MUSHROOM VELOUTÉ
with Blue Crab and Hazelnut Cream

The crabmeat in this soup is a delicious indulgence. Without the crabmeat you have a wonderful creamy asparagus and mushroom soup.

SOUP:

2	*pounds fresh asparagus*
1	*pound mushrooms*
½	*cup butter*
1	*medium yellow onion, peeled and diced*
½	*cup all-purpose flour*
4	*cups chicken stock or canned chicken broth*
2	*sprigs fresh thyme*
1	*bay leaf*
2	*cups cream or half-and-half*
	Sea salt
	Ground white pepper
	Pinch of fresh nutmeg
1	*pound lump crabmeat*

HAZELNUT CREAM:

½	*cup shelled hazelnuts*
4	*tablespoons unsalted butter at room temperature*
1	*cup heavy cream*

Trim the tough, woody bottoms from the asparagus spears and discard them. Cut off the tips and set them aside. Cut the spears into ¼-inch pieces. Wipe the mushrooms clean with a damp towel and thinly slice them. Melt the butter in a deep pot over medium-high heat. When the foam subsides, add the sliced mushrooms and stir well. Increase the heat to high and cook the mushrooms, stirring occasionally, until the edges have begun to brown. Stir in the onion and the asparagus spears, reduce the heat to medium, and cook, stirring now and then or until the vegetables have softened and begun to yield their juices. Stir in the flour and cook for another 2 or 3 minutes. Add the stock, thyme, and bay leaf. Bring the soup to a simmer and cook for 20 minutes. Purée the soup and strain it through a medium-mesh sieve. Rinse out the pot and return the soup to the pot. Add the cream, reheat, and season to taste with salt, white pepper, and nutmeg.

While the soup is simmering, bring a separate pot of water to a boil, salt it lightly, and drop in the asparagus tips. Cook them for only a minute if small and tender, for an additional minute if large. Drain the asparagus in a colander and drop them into a bowl of ice water to set the color. Drain again and set aside. If the asparagus tips are large, slice them in half lengthwise. Pick over the crabmeat for bits of shell and set aside.

To make the hazelnut cream, preheat the oven to 350°F. Spread the hazelnuts on a small sheet pan and roast them in the oven for 12 minutes, or until they are lightly browned and fragrant. If the nuts are still in their papery skins, rub them off with a clean towel. Grind the nuts in the work bowl of a food processor or in a spice grinder to a smooth paste. Scrape the paste into a small bowl and mix it with the softened butter. Whip the heavy cream until it forms soft peaks and then fold it into the butter-hazelnut mixture. Refrigerate the hazelnut cream until ready to serve the soup.

To serve, reheat the soup and stir in the crabmeat and asparagus tips. Ladle the soup into deep soup bowls and place a generous dollop of the hazelnut cream in the center of each.

MAKES 12 SERVINGS

BAHAMIAN CONCH CHOWDER
with Bird Pepper Hot Sauce

This recipe of Norman van Aken's was the chowder Louie's served when I started here in 1985. It's the standard by which I judge all conch chowders. We make it in small batches every day to ensure the high quality taste.

4	ounces smoked bacon (preferably slab bacon with the rind removed), diced	2	medium boiling potatoes, peeled and diced
1	medium white or yellow onion, peeled and diced	2	cups fish stock or water
		3	cups bottled clam juice
2	celery ribs, diced	1	pound cleaned conch meat, ground
1	each red, yellow, and green bell pepper, stemmed, seeded, and diced	1	sprig fresh basil or ½ teaspoon dried basil
1	jalapeño, stemmed, seeded, and minced	1	sprig fresh thyme or ½ teaspoon dried thyme
2	(10-ounce) cans plum tomatoes, cut up, with their juice	1	sprig fresh oregano or ½ teaspoon dried oregano
2	(10-ounce) cans tomato purée	1	bay leaf
		1	teaspoon crushed red pepper
			Tabasco

Place the diced bacon in a large soup pot or Dutch oven and stir while cooking over high heat until the fat is rendered and the bacon is browned and crisp. Add the diced onion, celery, bell peppers, and jalapeño. Stir well and continue cooking over high heat until the vegetables have begun to soften and take on a bit of color. Add the tomatoes, tomato purée, and potatoes and remove the pot from the heat. Place the fish stock and clam juice in a second pot and bring to a boil over high heat. Add the ground conch and stir well to break up any lumps. When the liquid returns to a boil, strain it through a medium-mesh sieve into the first pot. Set the conch aside. Return the first pot to medium-high heat and bring the liquid to a simmer. Tie the basil, thyme, oregano, and bay leaf in a square of cheesecloth and add it to the pot. Simmer the chowder for 20 minutes, or until the potatoes are cooked. Add the cooked conch and simmer for 5 more minutes. Remove the cheesecloth of herbs and season the soup with red pepper and Tabasco to taste. Serve with Bird Pepper Hot Sauce (page 100).

MAKES 10 TO 12 SERVINGS

CHILLED BUTTERMILK SOUP
with "The Best of Florida" Shellfish

Along with the extravagance of the shellfish, this soup is garnished with fresh chervil. Our herb grower says that in Florida, chervil—similar to parsley—will grow only from Turkey Day to Tax Day: That is fine for us because that coincides with the height of lobster and stone crab season. If chervil can't be found, parsley makes a reasonable substitute, or it could simply be omitted.

1	*pound jumbo Gulf shrimp*	1	*cup cooked barley*
2	*(6-ounce) Florida lobster tails in the shell*	½	*cup finely diced red onion*
1	*pound large stone crab claws (about 4)*		*Ground white pepper (optional)*
4	*navel oranges*		*Salt (optional)*
4	*cups low-fat buttermilk*	2	*tablespoons finely snipped fresh chives*
½	*cup Sour Orange Mustard (page 111)*	2	*tablespoons chervil leaves*

Bring 2 quarts of water to a boil over high heat. Add the shrimp and cook for 2½ minutes. Remove the shrimp with a slotted spoon and chill. When they are cold, shell and devein the shrimp and split them in half lengthwise. Wrap the lobster tails very tightly in plastic wrap, using about 2 feet of wrap for each tail. Drop the wrapped tails into the boiling water and cook for exactly 9 minutes. Remove the tails from the water and drop them into a bowl of ice water to chill thoroughly. When they are cold, remove the plastic wrap, take the meat from the shell, and cut it into 1-inch pieces. Crack the stone crab claws and carefully remove all of the meat from the shells. Keep all of the prepared shellfish well chilled. Cut the four oranges into fillets. Combine the buttermilk, mustard, barley, and onion in a mixing bowl. Season with pinches of ground white pepper and salt if necessary.

To serve, divide the shellfish among eight chilled soup bowls, mounding it in the center of each bowl. Pour the buttermilk soup around the shellfish, scatter the orange fillets over the top, and garnish with the chives and chervil.

MAKES 8 SERVINGS

BLACK BEAN PURÉE
with Little Ham Fritters

Black beans are typically used to make a hearty, country-style soup that is coarse in texture with diced peppers and onions and lots of cilantro. It's wonderful, but sometimes the occasion calls for something slightly more refined. This is a far cry from a typical black bean soup. It's smooth and velvety and elegant, with surprising hints of cinnamon and orange zest.

1	tablespoon olive oil
2	ounces smoked bacon, preferably slab bacon, rind removed, diced
4	garlic cloves, peeled, minced
1	small carrot, peeled, diced
4	ribs celery, diced
2	medium yellow onions, peeled, diced
1	green bell pepper, stemmed, seeded, diced
3	jalapeños, stemmed, seeded, minced
2	cups black beans, picked over, rinsed, and soaked overnight in 6 cups water
1	(1-inch) long cinnamon stick
1	strip of orange zest (½ inch by 3 inches)
1	bay leaf
½	plus ½ cup dry sherry
8	cups chicken stock or canned chicken broth

1	smoked ham hock
	Salt
	Pepper

LITTLE HAM FRITTERS:

1	smoked ham hock (leftover from the Black Bean Purée)
1	garlic clove, peeled
2	ounces smoked bacon, rind removed, chopped
¾	cup grated Parmesan cheese
1	cup dry breadcrumbs
2	extra large eggs
2	tablespoons Italian parsley, chopped
	A few scrapings of fresh nutmeg
¼	teaspoon fresh ground black pepper
2	cups vegetable oil (for frying)
	Sour cream for garnish

Heat the olive oil in a large soup pot or Dutch oven and add the bacon. Cook over high heat until the fat is rendered and the bacon is crisp. Add the garlic and stir. Immediately add the carrot, celery, onions, bell pepper, and jalapeños and stir well. Cook over high heat until the vegetables are beginning to brown and have softened slightly. Drain the beans and add them to the vegetables along with the cinnamon stick, orange zest, bay leaf, ½ cup dry sherry, chicken stock, and ham hock. Bring the liquid to a boil, reduce the heat, and cook at a slow simmer for 1½ hours, or until the beans are very tender. Remove the bay leaf, orange zest, cinnamon stick, and ham hock. Reserve the ham hock for the Little Ham Fritters. Purée the soup and strain it through a medium-mesh sieve. Rinse out the pot and return the soup to the pot and reheat. Season to taste with salt and pepper.

To make the Little Ham Fritters, remove the meat and fat from the ham hock and chop it fine. Discard the skin and bones. Set the meat aside. Place the garlic and bacon in the work bowl of a food processor and process until nearly smooth. Add the cheese, breadcrumbs, eggs, parsley, nutmeg, and pepper to the bowl. Process using short pulses, frequently scraping the sides of the bowl until the mixture forms a well-amalgamated paste. Add the chopped ham and process just long enough to mix it in. Shape the mixture into small, ½-inch balls and place them on a plate. Heat the vegetable oil in a saucepan to 360°F. Carefully add 10 or 12 fritters to the oil and cook until they are golden brown. Remove the fritters with a slotted spoon or skimmer and drain on paper towels. Keep them warm while you fry the remaining fritters.

To serve, reheat the soup, stir in the remaining ½ cup sherry and ladle the soup into wide-rimmed soup bowls. Garnish each bowl with 2 tablespoons of sour cream and 5 or 6 fritters.

MAKES 12 SERVINGS

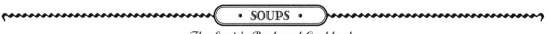
CHILLED CELERY ROOT SOUP
with Frozen Chèvre Cream

A discussion in the kitchen over whether a well-known chef's creation of goat cheese ice cream was inspiration or foolishness led to this soup and its unusual garnish.

SOUP:

1	pound celery root, peeled and cut into 1-inch pieces
2	large leeks, white and pale green parts only, trimmed, rinsed, and cut into 1-inch pieces
3	medium boiling potatoes, peeled and cut into 1-inch pieces
1	Granny Smith apple, peeled, cored, and cut into 1-inch pieces
4	cups chicken stock or canned chicken broth
2	sprigs fresh thyme
1	bay leaf
1	tablespoon sea salt or kosher salt
1	teaspoon ground white pepper
2	cups cream or half-and-half

FROZEN CHÈVRE CREAM:

1	cup heavy cream
½	pound chèvre
4	tablespoons roasted garlic purée
1½	teaspoons fresh thyme leaves
4	extra large egg yolks
4	tablespoons sugar
½	teaspoon sea salt or kosher salt
1	pinch of ground white pepper
2	tablespoons finely snipped fresh chives

To make the soup, combine the celery root, leeks, potatoes, apple, chicken stock, thyme, bay leaf, sea salt, and white pepper in a soup pot. Bring the mixture to a boil, reduce the heat, and simmer until all of the vegetables are very soft, about 30 minutes. Purée the soup and pass it through a medium-mesh sieve. Add the cream and chill the soup in the refrigerator.

To make the frozen chèvre cream, combine the cream, chèvre, garlic, and thyme in a small saucepan and stir over medium heat until the cheese has melted and the mixture is hot. Combine the egg yolks, sugar, salt, and pepper in a small mixing bowl and whisk them together well. Gradually whisk in the hot cream mixture and return everything to the saucepan. Cook over medium heat, stirring constantly, until the mixture is hot, the egg yolks have thickened, and the liquid thickly coats the spoon. Don't let it boil. Chill the mixture well and then freeze it in an ice cream machine following the manufacturer's directions.

To serve, ladle the soup into chilled, wide-rimmed soup bowls. Place a scoop of the chèvre cream in the center of each and garnish with the snipped chives.

MAKES 8 SERVINGS

CREAMY LEEK SOUP
with Oysters and Artichokes

There's no way around it: artichokes are a lot of work! But their sweet, nutty flavor and seductive texture make them well worth the effort. In the kitchen at Louie's Backyard we use a lot of artichokes, and anyone with time on his hands soon finds himself stripping thorny armor.

2	*large artichokes*
1	*pint shucked oysters with their liquor*
½	*cup butter*
1	*bunch leeks, white and pale green parts, trimmed, well rinsed, and sliced ¼-inch thick*
½	*cup all-purpose flour*
3	*cups fish or chicken stock*
2	*medium boiling potatoes, peeled and sliced (about 1 cup)*
2	*sprigs fresh thyme*
2	*cups cream or half-and-half*
	Salt
	Ground white pepper
	Freshly grated nutmeg

To trim the artichokes, cut the stem off even with the base and discard it. Snap back the leaves of the artichoke and peel them off (you may have to use scissors), leaving the meaty portion attached to the base of the artichoke. Keep snapping off leaves until the pale green center cone is exposed. Cut across the top of the artichoke to remove the center cone of leaves. With a sharp paring knife, trim away all of the dark green, fibrous outer portions of the artichoke base, but leave the choke intact. Place the artichokes in a pan with 4 cups of water and bring to a boil. Cook the artichokes for about 20 minutes or until a toothpick inserted in the thickest part will go through the artichoke with just the slightest resistance. A perfectly cooked artichoke has the same feel as a perfectly boiled potato—firm enough to slice and hold its shape, but not the least bit crunchy. Remove the artichokes to a bowl of ice water and chill them thoroughly to stop the cooking. When the artichokes are cool,

place them upside down on a cutting board and cut them into quarters. Remove the hairy choke from each quarter with a sharp paring knife, leaving the rim of leaf bases intact. Cut each quarter into four or five wedges and set aside.

Place the oysters with their liquor in a small saucepan and heat gently just until the edges of the oysters begin to curl. Drain the oysters and reserve them and their liquor separately. If the oysters are quite large, cut them into several pieces each. Melt the butter in a deep pot, add the sliced leeks, and cook, stirring some, until the leeks have softened and are fragrant. Stir in the flour and continue to cook for 2 or 3 minutes. Add the stock, the reserved oyster liquor, potatoes, and thyme; stir well and simmer the soup for 20 minutes or until the potatoes are very tender. Purée the soup and strain it through a medium-mesh sieve. Rinse out the pot, return the soup to the pot, and add the cream. Reheat the soup and season to taste with salt, white pepper, and nutmeg. Just before serving, stir in the reserved oysters and the pieces of artichoke.

MAKES 10 TO 12 SERVINGS

YELLOW PEPPER SOUP
with Avocado Cream

This soup can be made with red bell peppers, yellow bell peppers, or a combination of bell peppers. But when it's made with all yellow peppers, with its bright taste, it's like sunshine in a bowl.

5	large yellow bell peppers, ribs, stems, and seeds removed
2	leeks, white and pale green parts only, washed well
1	large Spanish onion, peeled
2	celery ribs
1	medium carrot, peeled
6	garlic cloves, peeled
6	tablespoons butter
6	tablespoons all-purpose flour
4	cups chicken stock or canned chicken broth
6	to 8 sprigs fresh thyme, tied with string, or 2 teaspoons dried thyme
1	cup heavy cream or half-and-half
4	teaspoons sea salt or kosher salt
1	teaspoon freshly ground black pepper
¼	teaspoon cayenne

AVOCADO CREAM:

1	ripe avocado, peeled and pitted
1	tablespoon fresh lemon juice
½	teaspoon sea salt or kosher salt
1	cup sour cream
20	large fresh basil leaves

Cut the peppers, leeks, onion, celery, and carrot into 1-inch pieces. Finely chop the garlic. Melt the butter in a large soup pot or Dutch oven. When the foam subsides, add the garlic and stir. Cook the garlic for 1 or 2 minutes, without letting it brown at all, and add the cut-up vegetables. Stir well. Cook the vegetables over medium-high heat, stirring occasionally, until they have softened some, have begun to give up some liquid, and are beginning to be fragrant. They shouldn't take on any color. Sprinkle the flour over the vegetables and stir again. Cook for about 5 minutes, still stirring occasionally to cook the flour, and then stir in the chicken stock or broth. Add the bouquet of thyme. Bring the liquid up to a simmer; then reduce the heat and cook gently for 30 minutes. Stir now and then with a wooden spoon to make sure nothing is sticking to the pot's bottom and scorching. When the vegetables are soft—test by trying to smash a piece of carrot against the side of the pot—remove the pan from the heat. Purée the soup, either in the pot with an immersion blender or in batches in a standard blender, and pour it through a medium-mesh sieve. Rinse the pot and return the soup to it. Add the cream or half-and-half and stir well. Reheat the soup and season with salt, black pepper, and cayenne.

To make the avocado cream, place the avocado, lemon juice, salt, sour cream, and basil leaves in the work bowl of a food processor and purée until smooth.

To serve, ladle the hot soup into wide-rimmed soup bowls. Put 2 or 3 tablespoons of the avocado cream in the center of each and swirl to make a spiral design. Or put the avocado cream into a squeeze bottle with a medium tip and "draw" a design in each bowl.

MAKES 8 SERVINGS (2 QUARTS)

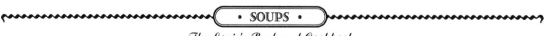
SHELLFISH AND HOT SAUSAGE GUMBO

This recipe for gumbo is close to what we serve at the restaurant, but gumbo is one of those great dishes that can't—and shouldn't—be made exactly the same way twice. In a restaurant like Louie's, there are always bits of exotica about: duck confit, smoked quail, or perhaps some whitewater clams or diver scallops. Any and all of these are likely to find their way to the gumbo pot. At the beach it might be surf clams or soft-shell crabs and some leftover ham. Once the basic recipe is mastered, the variations are endless.

6	to 8 cups rich chicken stock
1	pound fresh shrimp, peeled and deveined, cut into pieces if large, shells reserved
¾	cup vegetable oil
¾	cup all-purpose flour
2	medium yellow onions, peeled and diced
4	ribs celery, diced
1	red bell pepper, stemmed, seeded, and diced
1	yellow bell pepper, stemmed, seeded, and diced
3	jalapeños, stemmed, seeded, and diced
8	cloves garlic, peeled and minced
2	ripe red tomatoes, peeled, seeded, and diced
2	bay leaves
1	tablespoon salt
¾	teaspoon freshly ground black pepper
½	teaspoon cayenne
1	teaspoon dried thyme
1	teaspoon dried oregano
1	teaspoon dried basil
1	pound Andouille sausage, cut in ¼-inch slices
8	ounces fresh okra, cut in ¼-inch slices
1	pound jumbo lump crabmeat, picked over
1	pint shucked oysters with their liquor

Combine the chicken stock and shrimp shells in a deep pot, bring to a boil, lower the heat, and simmer for 20 minutes. Strain the stock, return it to the pot, and keep warm. Heat the vegetable oil over medium high heat in a heavy-bottomed soup pot or Dutch oven. Sift in the flour and begin stirring with a wire whisk. This will be the roux, the most crucial part of gumbo making, and will take about 25 to 30 minutes to complete. Keep stirring the mixture over medium-high heat with the whisk as it gradually darkens from a pale gold to the color of peanut butter and finally to a rich brown mahogany. The longer the roux cooks, the darker it gets and the deeper the flavor of the gumbo will be. When the roux is a rich dark brown and very fragrant, stir in one-half of the onions, celery, bell peppers, and jalapeños. They will hiss and sputter like mad and will look like they're coated with tar. Let them cook for about 3 minutes and then add the remaining vegetables. Cook for an additional 3 minutes and stir in the garlic. Stir and cook for about 3 minutes more and then stir in the tomatoes, bay leaves, salt, pepper, cayenne, thyme, oregano, and basil. The liquid from the tomatoes will combine with the roux forming a dark thick mass that may seem hard to stir, but keep stirring. Gradually add the hot stock, stirring well after each addition, and bring the gumbo to a simmer. After 15 minutes, add the sausage and the sliced okra. Simmer for 15 minutes more. Add the shrimp, crab, and oysters and simmer for 2 or 3 more minutes. Check the seasoning. Serve in deep bowls with plain white rice.

MAKES 20 TO 24 SERVINGS

TOMATILLO AND AVOCADO SOUP
with Sour Cream and Tortilla "Rajas"

R*ajas,* Spanish for "rags," is a term usually used to describe mild green chiles, peeled and cut into strips. We use the word on menus to describe tortillas torn or cut into strips and fried, which we use to garnish soups, salads, fish, and meat dishes.

2	*tablespoons butter*
2	*medium yellow onions, peeled and diced*
2	*medium carrots, peeled and diced*
3	*ribs celery, diced*
8	*cloves garlic, peeled and minced*
4	*jalapeños, stemmed, seeded, and chopped*
2	*pounds tomatillos, husks removed, rinsed well, and quartered*
6	*cups chicken stock or canned chicken broth*
4	*avocados, peeled, pit removed*
4	*tablespoons chopped fresh cilantro*
2	*cups heavy cream or half-and-half*
1	*tablespoon kosher salt or sea salt*
1	*teaspoon freshly ground black pepper*
1	*tablespoon cumin seed, toasted lightly and ground in a spice grinder*
4	*(6-inch) corn tortillas*
2	*cups vegetable oil (for frying)*
1	*teaspoon kosher salt or sea salt*
¼	*teaspoon cayenne*
2	*teaspoons cumin seed, toasted lightly and ground in a spice grinder*
1	*tablespoon fresh lime juice*
1	*cup sour cream*

Melt the butter in a heavy-bottomed pot or Dutch oven. Add the onions, carrots, celery, garlic, and jalapeños. Cook, stirring occasionally, for 10 minutes, until the vegetables have softened and are beginning to render their juices. They should "sweat" in the pot, not fry. Add the tomatillos and stir well. Cook until the tomatillos have released their liquid. Add the chicken stock and simmer for 20 to 30 minutes or until all of the vegetables are very soft. Add the avocados, cilantro, and cream. Purée the soup and pass it through a medium-mesh sieve. Rinse out the pot and return the soup to it. Season with the salt, pepper, and ground cumin and keep it warm. Cut the tortillas into a fine julienne. Heat the vegetable oil in a 2-quart saucepan to 360°F. When the oil is hot, add the tortilla strips and fry them, stirring so they cook evenly and are lightly browned and very crisp. Drain the tortilla strips on paper towels. Mix together the salt, cayenne, and ground cumin. Season the tortilla strips with the mixture. Stir the lime juice into the sour cream.

To serve, ladle the soup into warmed bowls, spoon some sour cream into the center of each, and garnish with the warm tortilla strips.

MAKES 12 SERVINGS

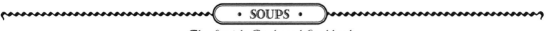
CHILLED CARROT SOUP
with Champagne Vinegar and Edible Flowers

We have a couple of determined souls in the Keys who fight the heat and humidity of "Zone 11" growing conditions to provide us herbs and edible flowers. If you're not lucky enough to have a source of insecticide-free blossoms, this soup would also be delicious garnished with finely snipped fresh chives, dill, or a chiffonade of basil.

3	*pounds young, sweet carrots, preferably with tops*	½	*cup plus 3½ cups spring water*
4	*leeks, white and pale green parts only, well washed*	1	*sprig fresh thyme*
		1	*cup flower "confetti"*
4	*shallots, peeled and sliced*		*Salt*
4	*tablespoons butter*		*A few grains of cayenne*
		2	*cups champagne*

Remove the tops from the carrots and reserve. Peel the carrots and cut them into 1-inch pieces. Thinly slice the leeks. Melt the butter in a heavy-bottomed pot with a tight-fitting lid and add the carrots, leeks, and shallots. Stir well to coat them with the butter. Add the ½ cup water and the thyme. Cover the pot and braise the vegetables over low heat for 20 minutes, until the carrots have softened. Stir occasionally and add additional water if necessary. The vegetables should never "fry." Add the remaining 3½ cups water, bring the soup to a simmer, and cook until the carrots are very tender. Purée the soup, pour it through a medium-mesh sieve and refrigerate it until thoroughly chilled.

While the soup is chilling, make the flower "confetti." Use a mixture of small roses, pansies, dianthus, and nasturtiums, or all one kind. Flowers with small petals work best. They must be insecticide free and freshly picked. Remove the calyxes from the flowers and place the petals in a small bowl. Chop enough of the fine leaves of the carrot tops to make 2 tablespoons. Mix the chopped greens with the flower petals.

When the soup is cold, season to taste with salt and cayenne. Stir in the champagne. Ladle the soup into pretty glass bowls and scatter the flower "confetti" over it.

MAKES 8 SERVINGS

CUBAN STYLE WHITE BEAN SOUP

This is much like the bean soups available in all of the island's Cuban restaurants. It's a hearty, meaty soup with beans *and* potatoes.

2	cups Great Northern beans, picked over and rinsed	8	cups chicken stock or canned chicken broth or water
2	ounces slab bacon, rind removed, diced	2	teaspoons dry oregano
		1	bay leaf
6	cloves garlic, peeled and minced	1	meaty ham bone or 2 ham hocks
2	medium yellow onions, peeled and diced	4	medium boiling potatoes, peeled and sliced ¼ inch thick
2	medium carrots, peeled and diced	4	tablespoons Italian parsley, chopped
3	ribs celery, diced		Salt
1	green bell pepper, stemmed, seeded, and diced		Black pepper
1	(10-ounce) can plum tomatoes, cut up, with their juice		Tabasco

Heat the Great Northern beans in a heavy-bottomed pot or Dutch oven over medium-high heat. Add the diced bacon and cook, stirring some, until the fat is rendered and the bacon is browned and crisp. Add the garlic and stir. Immediately add the onions, carrots, celery, and bell pepper and stir well to coat them with the fat. Cook over high heat, stirring, until the vegetables have softened and are beginning to brown. Add the tomatoes with their juice, stock, herbs, and ham bone. Bring the liquid to a boil, reduce the heat to a simmer, and cook gently for 45 minutes, stirring occasionally. If the soup becomes too thick, thin it with additional stock or water. Add the sliced potatoes and continue to cook until the potatoes and the beans are very tender, about 30 minutes more. Remove the ham bone or hocks from the soup. When they are cool enough to handle, take the meat from the bones and chop it well. Return the chopped ham to the soup. Discard the bones. Season the soup with the parsley and the salt, black pepper, and hot sauce to taste. Adjust the consistency with water or additional stock if necessary.

MAKES 12 SERVINGS

GAZPACHO

Roundsman Steven George, whose recipe this is, will sometimes enhance this cold soup with grilled and chilled shrimp or jumbo lump blue crabmeat.

3	cups tomato juice
1	cup chicken or beef broth
2	large, ripe tomatoes, seeded and cut into ½ inch dice
1	European cucumber, split, seeded and cut into ½ inch dice
1	yellow bell pepper, seeds and ribs removed, cut into ¼ inch dice
1	poblano pepper, seeds and ribs removed, cut into ¼ inch dice
1	red onion, peeled and cut into ¼ inch dice
4	scallions, roots trimmed and thinly sliced
½	teaspoon cayenne pepper
1	teaspoon freshly ground black pepper
1	teaspoon Tabasco sauce

Combine the tomato juice, broth, tomatoes, cucumber, bell pepper, poblano pepper, red onion, scallions, cayenne pepper, black pepper, and Tabasco sauce, in a non-reactive container and place the soup in the refrigerator for at least 2 hours. Serve very cold in chilled bowls.

MAKES 4 SERVINGS

SAUCES & ACCOMPANIMENTS

Romesco Sauce

Aïoli

Bird Pepper Hot Sauce

Sweet Soy Sauce

Bagna Cauda

Ponzu

Green Mango Sauce

Spicy Cashew Sauce

Hollandaise

Hot Pepper Jelly

Lemon Grass Pesto

Rye Croutons

Mango Chutney

Pomodoro Sauce

Red Pepper Rouille

Sweet and Sour Tomatoes

Roasted Garlic

Saffron-Pernod Butter

Spicy Mayonnaise

Papaya Salsa

Sour Orange Mustard

Jamaican Jerk Rub

ROMESCO SAUCE

Rustic, earthy, and incredibly versatile, this sauce is good with grilled or fried fish, grilled meats, and grilled or roasted vegetables.

2	*red ripe tomatoes (about 1 pound)*	20	*blanched almonds or 2 ounces sliced or slivered almonds*
1	*teaspoon plus 1½ cups extra virgin olive oil*	1	*(2-inch-thick) slice country bread or baguette*
2	*ancho chiles*	1	*teaspoon crushed red pepper*
1	*cup water*		*Salt*
6	*tablespoons red wine vinegar*		*Freshly ground black pepper*
10	*cloves garlic*		

Preheat the oven to 400°F. Remove the cores from the tomatoes, rub them with the 1 teaspoon olive oil, and place them in a pan in the oven for 20 to 25 minutes, or until the skins split and they are slightly blackened. Remove them from the oven.

Put the ancho chiles in a second pan and place them in the oven with the tomatoes. After 5 minutes remove the chiles from the oven (they should be puffed up and should smell wonderful), and when they are cool enough to handle, remove the stems and seeds and tear the chiles into large pieces. Place the pieces in a small bowl and cover them with the water and red wine vinegar. Set aside for at least 15 minutes, until the chiles have softened.

Heat ½ cup of the olive oil in a small skillet with the garlic cloves. Keep the heat low so the garlic cloves cook gently, becoming soft and pale golden in about 7 minutes. Remove the garlic cloves with a slotted spoon and set aside. Raise the heat under the skillet slightly and fry the almonds until they are golden brown. Remove the almonds with a slotted spoon and set them aside with the garlic. In the same oil, fry the slice of bread until it, too, is a nice golden brown on both sides. Set the bread aside with the garlic and any oil remaining in the pan.

In the jar of a blender or the work bowl of a food processor, combine the roasted tomatoes, the chiles with their soaking liquid, the garlic, almonds, bread, and red pepper. Blend to a coarse purée. With the machine running, drizzle in the remaining 1 cup of olive oil. Season to taste with salt and freshly ground black pepper. Store in the refrigerator.

MAKES 3 TO 4 CUPS

AÏOLI

This classic French garlicky mayonnaise can also be flavored with orange or lemon zest or chopped fresh herbs. It can be used as a dip for vegetables, or spread on a filet of fish before pressing it into breadcrumbs to make a flavorful sautéed crust.

2	*extra large egg yolks*
¼	*cup fresh lemon juice*
½	*teaspoon sea salt*
6	*cloves garlic, peeled and chopped (about 1 tablespoon)*
2	*cups olive oil*

Place the egg yolks, lemon juice, salt and garlic in the work bowl of a food processor and, with the machine running, drizzle in the olive oil to form a thick emulsion. Transfer to a small bowl and refrigerate.

MAKES 3 CUPS

BIRD PEPPER HOT SAUCE

This sauce will add a zing to steamed vegetables or cooked black or white beans. Bird peppers come from the Bahamas. They're very small, bright red, intensely hot chile peppers. Many Key Westers grow them in their yards, as much for the attractive shrub that bears them as for the chiles themselves.

1	*(750-mililiter) bottle Spanish sherry vinegar (about 3¼ cups)*
¼	*cup dried bird peppers or other very small, very hot, dried chiles*
4	*dried chipotle or morita chile peppers*

Pour the vinegar into a small saucepan and add the chile peppers. Warm the vinegar over low heat until it just begins to simmer. Remove from the heat and let the vinegar and chiles steep for 1 hour. Strain. Discard the chiles. Funnel the vinegar back into its bottle and store in a cool dark place.

MAKES ABOUT 3½ CUPS

SWEET SOY SAUCE

We use this condiment, derived from the Indonesian Ketjap Manis, in more ways than I can count. This recipe makes a large quantity, but the sauce keeps well and has so many uses that it seems silly to make less. However, the recipe can be divided (or multiplied) easily if a different size batch is desired.

4	*ounces fresh ginger, peeled, sliced ½ inch thick*
16	*cloves fresh garlic, peeled*
4	*jalapeños with seeds, stemmed and sliced ¼ inch thick*
8	*pieces star anise*
1	*cup plus 4 cups soy sauce (we like Kikkoman)*
4	*cups sugar*

Put the slices of ginger and the garlic cloves on a cutting board or countertop and hit them with the bottom of a heavy pot or the side of a cleaver to smash them. Combine them with the jalapeños and star anise in a small bowl and place the mixture near the stove. Measure the soy sauce and place it near the stove also. Put the sugar in a wide skillet with a very heavy bottom—cast iron is great—and place the pan over high heat. Stir the dry sugar with a wooden spoon until it has melted and caramelized. It should be a deep gold and smell great. Don't let the sugar burn. If lumps form, smash them against the bottom or sides of the pot with the wooden spoon, but don't fret about them. They will melt later. When the sugar has melted, remove the pan from the heat and carefully add the ginger, garlic, jalapeños, and anise. Hot sugar is a dangerous substance and care must be taken to stand well back from the pan to avoid splatters. Stir the mixture well and, again standing well back, pour in 1 cup of the soy sauce. The mixture will sputter wildly at first, then calm down as the temperature drops. Stir in the remaining 4 cups soy sauce. The mixture will look awful, black with big sticky lumps of ginger and chiles. Put the pan back on the heat, reduce it to medium, and cook, stirring occasionally, at a slow simmer for 15 minutes. The sugar then should have dissolved into the soy sauce. Stir and cook for a minute or two more if it hasn't. Carefully strain the mixture through a sieve into a clean jar. Discard the aromatics.

MAKES ABOUT 2 QUARTS

BAGNA CAUDA

Back in the very earliest days of Louie's Backyard, this unorthodox version of the classic Bagna Cauda was brought to every table at the beginning of the meal.

2	tablespoons unsalted butter	1	tablespoon flour
4	ounces anchovies	¼	teaspoon ground white pepper
3	tablespoons chopped fresh garlic	2	cups cream

Melt the butter in a small saucepan. Add the anchovies and the garlic and cook over medium heat, mashing the anchovies with the back of a wooden spoon until the mixture is very warm and fragrant. Stir in the flour and white pepper. Add the cream, increase the heat, and simmer until slightly thickened. Serve in a fondue pot surrounded by chunks of crusty bread and sliced raw vegetables for dipping.

MAKES 4 TO 6 SERVINGS

PONZU

This sauce has appeared on the menu in at least a dozen dishes: as a dressing for vegetable and noodle salads, a sauce for fried shrimp or seared tuna, or a dipping sauce for spring and summer rolls.

1	cup fresh-squeezed orange juice	2	tablespoons chopped cilantro
2	tablespoons fresh-squeezed lime juice	1	cup soy sauce
2	tablespoons fresh-squeezed lemon juice	½	cup Sweet Soy
2	tablespoons chopped garlic	4	tablespoons sesame seeds, black or white or a mixture, toasted
2	tablespoons chopped ginger	4	scallions, thinly sliced

In a large bowl combine the orange juice, lime juice, lemon juice, garlic, ginger, cilantro, soy sauce, Sweet Soy Sauce, sesame seeds, and scallions. Mix well.

MAKES ABOUT 3 TO 3½ CUPS

GREEN MANGO SAUCE

This sauce is wonderfully fresh and vibrant over grilled fish or chicken or used as a dip for spring rolls or steamed shrimp.

½	cup fresh lime juice	2	cloves garlic, finely chopped
½	cup Thai fish sauce	2	bird peppers, very finely chopped
½	cup water		
2	tablespoons rice vinegar	1	small green mango, peeled and grated (about ¾ cup)
4	teaspoons sugar		

Combine the lime juice, fish sauce, water, vinegar, sugar, garlic, peppers, and mango a mixing bowl or pitcher. Store in the refrigerator.

MAKES ABOUT 2½ CUPS

SPICY CASHEW SAUCE

This is a good all-purpose sauce for dipping, for noodles, for stir-fried vegetables, and more. Peanuts can be substituted for the cashews.

8	ounces unsalted cashews, roasted	2	tablespoons soy sauce
2	teaspoons chopped fresh ginger	1	tablespoon chile paste with garlic
2	teaspoons chopped garlic	2	tablespoons fresh lime juice
1	tablespoon sugar	1	cup water

Combine the cashews, ginger, garlic, sugar, soy sauce, chile paste, lime juice, and water in a blender and blend to a smooth creamy sauce. Transfer to a small bowl or a plastic squeeze bottle with a medium tip.

MAKES 2 CUPS

HOLLANDAISE

Although we're rarely content to leave a Hollandaise sauce alone—giving in to the urge to add something such as reduced orange juice or some smoky chile purée—it still must first be made properly, and properly made, it really doesn't need any embellishment.

6	extra large egg yolks	1½	cups warm, clarified butter
2	tablespoons fresh lemon juice	½	teaspoon sea salt
2	tablespoons water	⅛	teaspoon cayenne pepper

Beat the egg yolks, lemon juice, and water with a wire whisk in a medium mixing bowl until very light and frothy. Place the bowl over a pan of simmering water. The bottom of the bowl should not touch the water. Continue whisking the yolks, reaching all over the bottom of the bowl, until the whisk leaves a path that lets you glimpse the bottom of the bowl. Remove the bowl from the heat and, while whisking constantly, slowly drizzle in the clarified butter. Season the sauce with salt and cayenne and keep it warm.

MAKES ABOUT 2 CUPS

HOT PEPPER JELLY

This southern classic finds an unusual matchup with Japanese wasabi. It's still just as comfortable with some cream cheese "sittin' on a Ritz."

2	cups ground red bell pepper with juice	6½	cups sugar
		1½	cups cider vinegar
¼	cup dried red pepper flakes	2	pouches liquid fruit pectin

Combine the ground peppers, pepper flakes, sugar, and vinegar in a wide, deep pan and bring to a boil. Remove from the heat and allow to rest for 20 minutes, stirring occasionally. Return the pan to the heat and bring to a hard boil—one that can't be stirred down—for 2 minutes. Remove from the heat, strain into a bowl, and stir in the pectin. Skim the surface for 2 or 3 minutes. Pour into clean glass canning jars, cover, and refrigerate, or seal according to the manufacturer's instructions.

MAKES ABOUT 1 QUART

LEMON GRASS PESTO

This keeps well in the refrigerator, and besides its use in the Mussels Steamed in Coconut Milk, it makes a great rub for chicken or fish.

¼	*cup finely sliced lemon grass, the pale edible parts*
6	*cloves garlic, peeled and roughly chopped*
½	*cup fresh ginger, peeled and roughly chopped*
4	*shallots, peeled and roughly chopped*
8	*jalapeños, stemmed, seeded, and chopped*
2	*poblano peppers, stemmed, seeded, and chopped*
1	*cup chopped fresh cilantro, leaves and stems*
2	*tablespoons sea salt or kosher salt*
¼	*cup canola oil*

Combine the lemon grass, garlic, ginger, shallots, jalapeño and poblano peppers, cilantro, salt, and oil in the jar of a blender and process to a fine purée. Store in a covered container in the refrigerator.

MAKES 2½ TO 3 CUPS

RYE CROUTONS

These will keep for several days in a sealed plastic bag and are as good tossed into a green salad as they are sprinkled on the Beer and Cheddar soup.

8	*slices good, hearty rye bread with seeds*
4	*tablespoons melted butter*

Preheat the oven to 350°F. Trim the crusts from the bread and cut into ¼-inch cubes. Place the cubes in a bowl and toss with the butter to coat evenly. Spread the croutons on a sheet pan and bake for 8 to 10 minutes or until nicely browned and crisp.

MAKES ABOUT 4 CUPS

MANGO CHUTNEY

June is the height of the mango season in the Keys. In good years there are mangos everywhere, bouncing and rolling down the tin roofs, in baskets for sale at every corner grocery, left in bags on the front porch by generous neighbors. There are so many that we can't keep up, so we "put up." This chutney is good with any kind of pork or ham and of course it's the perfect accompaniment for curry.

3	mangoes, peeled and diced, about 6 cups		½	teaspoon sea salt
2	cups cider vinegar		1½	teaspoons ground cinnamon
1	cup granulated sugar		1	tablespoon minced fresh ginger
1	cup dark brown sugar		¼	teaspoon ground cloves
1	cup chopped yellow onion		1	teaspoon ground allspice
3	cloves garlic, peeled and finely chopped		2	teaspoons whole yellow mustard seeds
½	teaspoon freshly ground black pepper		½	cup raisins
1½	teaspoons crushed red pepper		½	cup Zante currants
			4	Granny Smith apples, peeled, cored, and diced

Combine the mangos, vinegar, sugars, onion, garlic, peppers, salt, cinnamon, ginger, cloves, allspice, mustard seeds, raisins, currants, and apples in a large, nonreactive pot, cover, and leave overnight at room temperature. The next day bring the mixture to a boil over medium-high heat. Reduce the heat to medium and simmer the chutney for 30 to 40 minutes, stirring occasionally until the liquid is syrupy and the fruits are translucent. Cool the chutney and store it, covered, in the refrigerator, or pack it while hot into sterile canning jars and process according to the manufacturer's instructions.

MAKES 6 PINTS

POMODORO SAUCE

This sauce is great for pizza, for pasta, or for tossing with sautéed shrimp. Roasting the tomatoes deepens their flavor.

6	*large red ripe tomatoes*
¼	*plus ¼ cup olive oil*
1	*tablespoon chopped garlic*
6	*branches fresh thyme*
	Salt and freshly ground black pepper

Preheat the oven to 400°F. Cut the core from the tomatoes and cut them in half horizontally. Coat the bottom of a shallow roasting pan with ¼ cup of the olive oil. Sprinkle the garlic over the oil, then scatter the thyme branches over the garlic. Season the cut sides of the tomatoes with salt and pepper and place them, cut side down, over the garlic and thyme. Drizzle the remaining olive oil over the tomatoes and place them on the middle rack in the oven. Roast the tomatoes for 30 minutes, until the skins have blistered and browned and the tomatoes are soft. Remove the tomatoes from the oven and allow to cool slightly. When cool enough to touch, pull the blistered skin away from the tomato flesh and discard it. Pick out the thyme branches and discard them. Transfer the remaining contents of the roasting pan to a small sauce pan, taking care to scrape the roasting pan well. Simmer the mixture for 10 to 12 minutes, mashing the tomatoes against the sides of the pot with a wooden spoon or crushing them with a potato masher into a coarse textured purée. Taste the tomatoes for salt and pepper and add more if necessary.

MAKES 12 SERVINGS

RED PEPPER ROUILLE

This is another very useful sauce. It's wonderful drizzled over grilled or sautéed fish, with grilled skinless chicken breasts, or even with hard-boiled eggs!

2	slices (about 2 ounces) country bread, crust removed	24	large fresh basil leaves
4	jalapeños, stemmed and seeded	10	medium cloves garlic, peeled
4	red bell peppers, roasted, peeled, and seeded	½	cup extra virgin olive oil
			Sea salt
			Freshly ground pepper

Place the slices of bread in a small bowl and cover them with cold water. Drain the bread, squeeze it gently between your hands, and place it in the work bowl of a food processor with the jalapeños, the bell peppers, the basil, and the garlic. Process the mixture to a coarse purée. Drizzle in the olive oil with the machine running. Season to taste with salt and freshly ground pepper. Transfer to a small bowl or jar and refrigerate up to 5 days.

MAKES ABOUT 2 CUPS

SWEET AND SOUR TOMATOES

As versatile as ketchup, this is another condiment worth keeping around.

6	cups canned Italian plum tomatoes, cut into medium pieces, with their juice	½	cup fresh garlic, peeled and finely chopped
½	cup fresh ginger, peeled and finely chopped	1	cup sugar
		1	cup rice vinegar

Combine the tomatoes, ginger, garlic, sugar, and vinegar in a heavy-bottomed saucepan or preserving pan and bring to a boil. Reduce the heat and simmer gently, stirring occasionally, for 45 minutes or until the mixture has reduced to a thick jam. Transfer to clean glass jars, cover, and store in the refrigerator.

MAKE 6 SERVINGS

ROASTED GARLIC

The flavor of garlic becomes mellow and sweet when it's roasted slowly in olive oil. They can be used to flavor sauces and salad dressings or gratins and compound butters; they're endlessly useful.

2	cups garlic cloves, peeled
2	cups olive oil
1	branch fresh thyme

Preheat the oven to 350°F. Combine the garlic, oil, and thyme in a small baking dish. Cover the dish with foil and place it in the oven for 30 minutes. After 30 minutes, remove the foil and check to see if the garlic is tender. It should be a very pale gold and tender when pierced with a fork. Let the garlic cool in the oil and strain it. Discard the thyme branch. Reserve the garlic cloves and garlic oil in separate containers in the refrigerator.

MAKES 2 CUPS ROASTED GARLIC AND 2 CUPS GARLIC OIL

SAFFRON-PERNOD BUTTER

This compound butter is used to make the Mussels Steamed with Saffron, Tomatoes, and Israeli Couscous. It is also good over any grilled fish or tossed with steamed vegetables.

½	cup chopped shallots	½	teaspoon saffron threads
¼	cup chopped garlic	¼	cup chopped Italian parsley
½	cup dry white wine	1	pound unsalted butter at room temperature
¼	cup Pernod		

Combine the shallots, garlic, wine, Pernod, saffron, and parsley in a small saucepan and cook until the liquids have nearly evaporated. Scrape the mixture into a mixing bowl and allow it to cool. Add the softened butter to the bowl and mix everything together thoroughly.

Wrap the butter in parchment paper or plastic wrap, forming a log about 2 inches in diameter. Refrigerate for 1 week or freeze for up to 1 month.

MAKES 3 CUPS

SPICY MAYONNAISE

This is our adaptation of a sushi bar staple. It pairs beautifully with tuna, whether the fish is grilled, pan-seared, or not cooked at all.

2	extra large egg yolks	1	tablespoon rice vinegar
1	tablespoon chopped fresh ginger	2	cups canola oil
1	tablespoon soy sauce	2	tablespoons chile paste with garlic

Put the egg yolks in the work bowl of a food processor with the ginger, soy sauce, and vinegar. Turn on the machine and slowly add the oil to form a thick emulsion. When all of the oil has been incorporated, add the chile paste. Taste the sauce. It should be quite spicy. Add more chile paste if needed. Transfer the sauce to a plastic squeeze bottle with a medium tip or a small bowl and refrigerate.

MAKES 2½ CUPS

PAPAYA SALSA

This colorful salsa brightens any Caribbean dish.

1	large papaya, ripe but still firm, peeled and cut into ½ inch cubes	½	small red onion, peeled and diced
2	jalapeño peppers, stemmed, seeded and minced	¼	cup chopped fresh cilantro
½	red bell pepper, stemmed, seeded and diced	2	limes, juiced
			Salt and freshly ground pepper

In a large bowl combine the papaya, jalapeno peppers, red bell peppers, red onion, cilantro, lime juice, and salt and pepper to taste. Refrigerate to combine flavors (about 1 hour). Serve with the Jamaican Jerk-Rubbed Chicken or other Caribbean dish.

MAKES ABOUT 4 CUPS

SOUR ORANGE MUSTARD

This concoction is another of our staples, always on hand. We use it to flavor sauces, to make mustard sauce for stone crab, and to dress fish sandwiches. If sour oranges are unavailable, any other varieity will do; just cut back the sugar slightly.

1	cup whole yellow mustard seed	¼	cup sugar
¼	cup dry mustard (we use Colman's)	1	tablespoon sea salt
1	cup water	2	tablespoons grated sour orange zest
1½	cups rice vinegar	½	cup sour orange juice
½	cup honey	1	tablespoon ground coriander seed

Using a spice grinder, grind the whole yellow mustard seeds to a fine powder. Mix the ground seeds, dry mustard, and water together in a small bowl and set aside for an hour or more, stirring two or three times as it sits. Transfer the contents of the bowl to a blender and add the vinegar, honey, sugar, salt, orange zest and juice, and coriander seed. Blend to a smooth consistency. Put in a glass container and store in the refrigerator.

MAKES ABOUT 6 CUPS

Ben Harris, Senior Waiter

Representing Louie's Backyard in the annual Florida Keys Seven Mile Bridge Run (from mile marker 47 to 40), Ben Harris has been at the restaurant just about as long as Doug Shook. He came in 1986, followed shortly by his brother Tomy; the two of them have been fundamental to the Louie's experience ever since.

"We are not a young group," he says of the waitstaff. "One time we added up how much experience there was in the dining room, and it came to centuries. That's a good thing—for us and for the regulars who come to Louie's. They know us, and we know them. For those of us who have been part of it so long, Louie's is not a stop on the way to somewhere else. It is our home and our family. We fight like brothers and sisters, and we hug like brothers and sisters. What most of us appreciate about this place is that the rules bend and flow. It isn't corporate. The owners are here; you can talk to them face-to-face."

Ben loves life in Key West, although he has seen it get significantly more expensive during his tenure as house prices have skyrocketed. Despite the high cost of shelter, he points out that when you live in Key West you have no heating bill. Furthermore, life is so casual that "your dry cleaning bill is zilch;" and while many people arrive in a car, "When their car breaks down, they just don't bother to replace it. You can get along here perfectly well without one. Yes, a house is more expensive on Key West. But the living is easy."

Donna D'Amato, Waitress

"Being Italian, I have the gift of walking, working, and gabbing all at the same time," says Donna D'Amato, who started waiting tables at Louie's Backyard fifteen years ago. "I wind up training most of the new people who hit the floor here. We are taught certain basic house rules, but we're all allowed to have our own style. That is the Louie's way."

Donna came to Key West in 1979. After working on the construction crew that built the approaches to the Seven Mile Bridge, she became headwaitress at Martha's restaurant. When one of her trainees there, Ben Harris, came to Louie's in 1986, he managed to get her a job at the newly reopened beachside restaurant. "In those days, someone had to die or move away for you to get a job at Louie's," Donna recalls. "This was—and it still is—just about the best restaurant to work in. I took a pay cut to come here, but I haven't regretted it. You deal with people who basically are thrilled to be in Key West, thrilled to be dining where they are dining. As for myself, how could I not like working here?" she asks, pointing to the crystalline blue ocean waters just beyond Louie's open-air dining room. "Look at my office!"

JAMAICAN JERK RUB

There are as many recipes for jerk rubs as there are for barbecue sauce. Some are dry, some are insanely hot. This one is fresh and flavorful. Be careful with the hot sauce though, adding a little at a time until the marinade is as hot as you like it. It's also great for pork, shrimp, and firm-fleshed fish.

1	cup orange juice
10	whole allspice berries
3	tablespoons chopped fresh cilantro
3	tablespoons chopped fresh thyme leaves
3	tablespoons chopped fresh oregano
3	tablespoons chopped Italian parsley
1	bunch scallions, trimmed and chopped
12	cloves garlic, peeled and roughly chopped
4	teaspoons kosher salt
1	teaspoon freshly ground black pepper
4	tablespoons Jamaican Scotch Bonnet hot sauce, such as Matouk's
4	tablespoons Creole mustard
2	tablespoons sherry vinegar

To make the jerk rub, combine the orange juice and allspice berries in a small saucepan and cook over medium heat until the juice is reduced to ¼ cup. Scrape the mixture into the work bowl of a food processor and add the cilantro, thyme, oregano, parsley, scallions, garlic, salt, pepper, hot sauce, mustard, and sherry vinegar. Process the mixture to a coarse purée. Transfer the mixture to a glass container and store it in the refrigerator

MAKES ABOUT 3 CUPS

Relax and come on in.

Welcome to Louie's.

The view from Louie's back porch is marvelous.

The Afterdeck bar is the perfect setting for a cocktail before dinner.

Key West's famous
Duval Street.

The libertine climate of Key West lends itself to much creativity.

Once the favored drink of Havana hipsters, the Mojito is a Louie's specialty.

Boston Lettuce and Watercress with Maytag Blue Cheese, Apples, and Spiced Pecans

*Grilled Tuna with Ginger Butter Sauce, Roasted Shiitakes, and
Sweet and Sour Tomatoes*

*Grilled Annatto-Rubbed Grouper
with Black Beans and Mango Salsa*

Chilled Gulf Shrimp with Cucumber Ribbons and Papaya-Chile Ice

Gulf Shrimp with Bacon, Mushrooms, and Stone-Ground Grits

Grilled Gulf Shrimp and Chorizo Sausage with Peppers, Onions, and Sherry Vinegar

You cannot make a true Key lime pie without limes from the Florida Keys.

Louie's makes its Key lime pie with a ginger snap crust.

Evenings are magical on the Afterdeck.

Good night from Louie's

SIDE
DISHES

Black Beans

Fried Ripe Plantains

Bacon Sage Potatoes

Gratin of Sweet and White Potatoes

Sweet Corn Pudding

Roasted Garlic Mashed Potatoes

Stone-Ground Grits

Fried Plantain Chips

Sweet Potato & Plantain Mash

Tostones

Wild Mushroom Bread Pudding

Yellow Rice

Zucchini Spoonbread

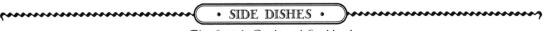
BLACK BEANS

Epazote is a Mexican herb that's used in the Yucatan, particularly to flavor black beans. Our "herb lady," Doris, grows it for us. It has a distinctive, almost harsh flavor when raw that mellows as it cooks. Use it if you can find it, but these beans will be delicious without it, too.

4	*cups black beans, picked over and rinsed*
¼	*pound slab bacon, with skin, in one piece*
1	*large yellow onion, peeled and diced*
2	*tablespoons chopped garlic*
3	*quarts water*
4	*sprigs Epazote, tied together with string (optional)*
½	*cup chopped fresh cilantro*
1	*tablespoon sherry vinegar*
1	*tablespoon sea salt, or to taste*

Combine the beans, bacon, onion, garlic, water, and epazote in a large, deep pot with a heavy bottom. Place over medium-high heat and bring to a boil. Turn the heat down to medium and simmer the beans, stirring occasionally, for approximately 90 minutes, depending on the age of the beans. Add boiling water to the pot if the level of the liquid threatens to drop below the level of the beans. When the beans are tender to the bite, stir in the cilantro, vinegar, and salt. Remove the piece of slab bacon from the pot and when it is cool enough to handle, finely chop it, skin and all. Return the chopped bacon to the bean pot. Cook for a few more minutes to blend the flavors. Serve or cool and refrigerate for up to 4 days.

MAKES 12 SERVINGS

FRIED RIPE PLANTAINS

Chiquita Banana said,"When they are flecked with brown and have a golden hue, that is when bananas are just right for you." But when a plantain is ripe, it's gone past the golden stage to nearly black. That's when enough of the starch has converted to sugar to allow the fruit to be cut into thick slices and gently sautéed. They're perfect with pork and even better with duck.

2	*very ripe plantains*
1	*cup all-purpose flour*
2	*teaspoons ground cinnamon*
1	*teaspoon sea salt*
½	*teaspoon freshly ground pepper*
4	*tablespoons unsalted butter*

Peel the plantains as you would peel a banana and slice them crosswise on the bias into ½-inch slices. Combine the flour, cinnamon, salt, and pepper and mix well. Dredge each plantain slice in the seasoned flour. Heat the butter in a wide skillet or sauté pan and when it has melted, add as many plantain slices as will fit without crowding the pan. Cook for 2 to 3 minutes or until golden brown on the bottom and then turn the slices over and brown the other side. Drain the slices on paper towels and repeat with the remaining plantains. Serve hot.

MAKES 4 TO 6 SERVINGS

BACON SAGE POTATOES

These potatoes were designed to complement the horseradish and roasted garlic flavors of Brendan's Horseradish-Crusted Snapper (page 160), but they're good enough to make for their own sake.

¼	*pound smoked slab bacon, rind removed, diced*
2½	*pounds Yukon Gold potatoes, scrubbed and cut into 1-inch pieces*
2	*ounces unsalted butter*
4	*tablespoons chopped fresh sage*
½	*cup milk*
	Salt
	Freshly ground black pepper

Cook the bacon in a small skillet until the fat is rendered and the bacon is browned and crisp. Put the potatoes in a large pot with water to cover them by 1 inch and boil them for 20 minutes or until they're very tender. Drain the potatoes well and return them to the pot. Add the butter, sage, milk, and bacon to the pot. Mash the potatoes well with a potato masher. Reheat them over medium heat if necessary, season well with the salt and pepper to taste, and serve hot.

MAKES 6 SERVINGS

GRATIN OF SWEET AND WHITE POTATOES
with Basil and Pine Nuts

Dense, rich, and full of surprising flavors, these potatoes are good with any grilled or roasted meats. We've been serving them off and on since 1985.

4	cloves Roasted Garlic (page 109)
6	extra large egg yolks
2	cups cream
1	small red onion, peeled and thinly sliced
1	jalapeño, stemmed, seeded, and thinly sliced
1	bunch basil, stems removed, leaves cut into fine strips
½	cup pine nuts, lightly toasted
	Sea salt
	Freshly ground pepper
3	Idaho potatoes (about 1½ pounds)
3	sweet potatoes (about 1½ pounds)

Preheat the oven to 375°F. In the bottom of a 9 x 13-inch baking dish, mash the roasted garlic cloves and spread them all over the inside of the dish. Beat the egg yolks in a small bowl and add the cream. Combine the yolks and cream thoroughly. Have the onion, jalapeño, basil, pine nuts, and salt and pepper prepared and at hand. Peel one of the Idaho potatoes and slice it nearly paper thin on a mandoline. Place the potatoes in a single, overlapping layer in the baking dish. Season with salt and pepper and evenly distribute one-fifth of the onion, jalapeño, basil, and pine nuts over the layer. Peel one of the sweet potatoes and follow the same procedure. Repeat with the remaining potatoes and seasonings, ending with a layer of sweet potato. Pour the custard over the potatoes. Press on them with your hand to submerge the potatoes in the custard. Cover the dish with buttered foil and bake for 90 minutes. Remove the foil and continue baking for 20 to 30 minutes longer or until the top of the gratin is nicely browned and a knife penetrates the center with no resistance. Let the gratin rest for 10 or 15 minutes before serving.

MAKES 6 TO 8 SERVINGS

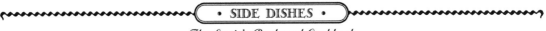
SWEET CORN PUDDING

This one is Southern. It's delicious with a grilled, rib-eye steak.

6	*ears sweet white or yellow corn*
5	*extra large eggs*
¾	*cup cream*
½	*cup milk*
¼	*pound Jack cheese, grated*
1	*tablespoon freshly chopped parsley or cilantro*
½	*teaspoon sea salt*
¼	*teaspoon freshly ground black pepper*

Preheat the oven to 325°F. Cut the kernels from the corn with a sharp knife. Turn the knife over and scrape the cut cobs with the back of the knife to extract all of the pulp and milk. Set aside 1 cup of the corn kernels. Put the remaining corn, with its juice, in a blender and process it to a smooth purée. In a bowl beat the eggs. Stir in the corn purée, the reserved kernels, cream, milk, cheese, and the herbs. Season with the salt and pepper. Pour the corn custard into a buttered, 6-cup baking dish, place the dish in a larger pan, and add hot water to come halfway up the sides. Bake for 1 hour or until the top of the pudding is lightly browned.

MAKES 6 SERVINGS

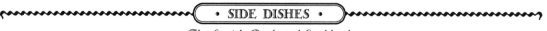
ROASTED GARLIC MASHED POTATOES

Frank Collins, who is the master of the grill at Louie's Backyard, is also the master of the mashed potato. This version is his best.

2½	*pounds Yukon gold potatoes*
½	*cup Roasted Garlic (page 109)*
½	*cup butter*
¾	*cup cream*
	Sea salt
	Freshly ground black pepper

Scrub the potatoes and cut them, with their skins, into 2-inch pieces. Place them in a deep pan, cover with water, and cook for 20 minutes or until the potatoes are tender. Drain the potatoes well, return them to the pot, and place the pot over medium-low heat. Stir the potatoes and cook for a few minutes to dry them out. Add the garlic, butter, and cream to the pot and mash the potatoes with a potato masher or sturdy wire whisk. A few lumps make the potatoes authentic. Season to taste with salt and pepper and serve hot.

MAKES 6 TO 8 SERVINGS

STONE-GROUND GRITS
with Cheddar Cheese

Real stone-ground grits are very different from the quick-cooking grocery store variety. In the restaurant a customer will sometimes tell the waiter, "I don't like grits." And the waiter will always reply, "But you haven't tried *these* grits."

1½	cups stone-ground grits (we use grits from Logan Turnpike Mill)	2	teaspoons salt
3¾	cups milk	2	cups grated sharp white Cheddar
3¾	cups water	½	teaspoon cayenne

In a deep, heavy-bottomed pot, combine the grits with the milk, water, and salt. Place over medium heat and cook, stirring often, for 45 minutes or until the grits have become a soft, thick porridge. Stir in the Cheddar and cayenne.

MAKES 6 SERVINGS

FRIED PLANTAIN CHIPS

Plantains can be sliced into thin ovals with a knife, but they must be very thinly sliced to achieve the proper crisp texture. Long, lengthwise slices are more eye-catching and appetizing.

2	green plantains
6	cups canola oil, for frying
	Sea salt

Peel the plantains. Slice them with a mandoline into nearly paper-thin, lengthwise slices. Place the slices in a bowl of cold water as they are cut. Heat the canola oil to 375°F in a wide, deep pot. Drain the plantain slices well and drop them, one at a time to prevent them from sticking together, into the oil. Fry for 3 or 4 minutes until the plantains are browned and crisp. Drain on paper towels. Sprinkle with salt to taste and serve hot or at room temperature.

MAKES 4 TO 6 SERVINGS

SWEET POTATO & PLANTAIN MASH

The plantains for this must be very, very ripe or they won't mash, even after baking. We usually serve this with grilled meats, but it's been seen on plates with grilled fish too.

2	*pounds medium sweet potatoes (about 4)*
2	*very ripe plantains*
6	*tablespoons butter*
6	*tablespoons milk*
	Sea salt
	Freshly ground black pepper

Preheat the oven to 400°F. Prick the sweet potatoes several times with a fork and place them on a baking sheet in the oven for 45 to 60 minutes, depending on their size, until they are very soft. Place the plantains, in their skins, in the oven with the sweet potatoes for the final 30 minutes of cooking time or until they are blackened and bursting in their skins. Peel the potatoes and plantains while hot and place them in a bowl. Mash them with a potato masher or electric mixer, working in the butter and milk. Season them with the salt and pepper. Reheat the mash over medium-low heat if necessary and serve hot.

MAKES 6 TO 8 SERVINGS

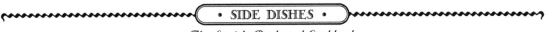
TOSTONES

Plantains look like giant bananas, but they're starchier, less sweet, and they need to be cooked to be enjoyable. How they're cooked depends on how ripe they are. This is a recipe for green, not-ripe plantains.

---

2   *large green plantains*

4   *cups canola oil, for frying*

1   *lime*

     Sea salt

Peel the plantains by cutting a slit down one side and then pulling the thick, bark-like skin away with your fingers. Cut them on a slight bias into ½- to ¾ -inch crosswise slices. Heat the canola oil in a suitable pot to 350°F. Add half of the plantain slices and cook them for about 7 minutes or until they are just barely tender when pierced with a fork. Remove them from the oil with a slotted spoon and drain on paper towels. Repeat with the remaining slices. One at a time, put the plantain slices on a cutting board and press on them with the side of a cleaver or the bottom of a small heavy pot. The sides of each slice should break and spread to about twice its original diameter and less than half an inch thick. Increase the temperature of the cooking oil to 375°F. When it is hot, slip in 5 or 6 slices of plantain and fry them for 3 or 4 minutes or until they are browned and crisp on the edges. Drain them on paper towels and repeat with the remaining slices. When all of the plantain slices have been fried, squeeze the lime juice over them, sprinkle them with salt, and serve them hot with a tomato salsa or Green Mango Sauce (page 103)

MAKES 6 TO 8 SERVINGS

WILD MUSHROOM BREAD PUDDING

Frequently the side dishes get as much—or more—attention as the main item on the plate. This is a favorite. It pairs well with most meats and with fish as well. It's fine, too, by itself as a vegetarian entrée.

1	tablespoon butter
1	large yellow onion, peeled and thinly sliced
1	teaspoon chopped fresh garlic
2	teaspoons chopped fresh thyme
¼	cup dry white wine
1	pound mushrooms, a mixture of farm mushrooms, shiitakes, and portobellos, trimmed, wiped clean, and thinly sliced
2	tablespoons olive oil
	Sea salt
	Freshly ground black pepper

CUSTARD MIXTURE:

3	extra large eggs
2	cups milk
2	tablespoons finely snipped chives or sliced scallions
1	teaspoon sea salt
1	tablespoon butter
½	loaf good country bread, crust removed, sliced ¾-inch thick
2	cups grated cheese, Parmesan, Jack, Gruyère, Asiago, Cheddar, or a mixture

---

Preheat the oven to 375°F. Melt the butter in a large sauté pan over medium-high heat. Add the onion, garlic, and thyme and cook, stirring until the onion begins to soften. Pour the white wine into the pan and continue to cook until the wine has evaporated. Stir in the mushrooms and the oil and continue to cook until the mushrooms release their liquid and it, too, has mostly evaporated. Season the mushroom mixture with the salt and pepper to taste.

For the custard mixture, beat the eggs lightly and stir in the milk, chives or scallions, and the 1 teaspoon salt. Butter a 9 x 9-inch glass baking dish. Arrange the slices of bread, cutting them to fit if necessary, to cover the bottom of the dish. Spread the mushroom and onion mixture over the bread and cover the mushrooms with half of the cheese. Arrange another layer of bread over the cheese. Pour in the custard mixture, pressing gently with your hands to help the bread absorb it. Spread the remaining cheese over the custard-soaked bread. Cover the dish with buttered foil and bake for 20 minutes. Remove the foil and continue baking for 10 to 15 minutes longer or until the pudding is puffed and browned.

MAKES 6 TO 8 SERVINGS

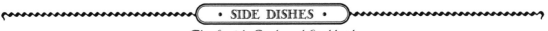
YELLOW RICE

Most yellow rice is colored with turmeric, safflower, or even artificial colors, which add little, if any, flavor. Not this one. This is robust with the color and flavor of saffron.

2	*tablespoons canola oil*
1	*small yellow onion, peeled and diced, about 1 cup*
2	*teaspoons chopped fresh garlic*
2	*ribs celery, trimmed and diced*
1	*jalapeño, stemmed, seeded, and minced*
½	*small red bell pepper, stemmed, seeded, and diced*
1	*tablespoon hot paprika*
⅛	*teaspoon cayenne pepper*
1	*teaspoon saffron threads*
2	*teaspoons sea salt*
2	*cups long grain rice*
4	*cups water*
2	*tablespoons unsalted butter*

Heat the oil in a 2-quart saucepan with a tight-fitting lid. When it is hot, add the onion, garlic, celery, and peppers. Cook the mixture, stirring occasionally, until the vegetables are soft and fragrant and have begun to brown on the edges. Stir in the paprika, cayenne, saffron, and salt and cook for another minute. Add the rice, stirring well to coat each grain with the vegetables and oil. Add the water, stir well again, and bring the mixture to a boil. Reduce the heat so the liquid barely simmers, cover the pot, and cook for 15 minutes or until all of the liquid has been absorbed and the rice is tender. Stir the butter into the rice and serve.

MAKES 6 TO 8 SERVINGS

ZUCCHINI SPOONBREAD

This sounds like a southern dish, and with its light sweetness, it seems like one too. Its origins, however, are Mexican. Serve it with pork chops or next to grilled or sautéed fish with a fruit salsa.

2	*pounds zucchini, trimmed and grated*
1½	*cups all-purpose flour*
½	*cup cornstarch*
1½	*teaspoons baking powder*
1	*teaspoon plus extra sea salt*
½	*pound unsalted butter, room temperature*
4	*extra large eggs*
¼	*cup sugar*
1	*cup sour cream*
2	*tablespoons fresh lime juice*
2	*teaspoons ground cumin*
	Freshly ground black pepper
½	*cup pine nuts*

Preheat the oven to 350°F. Squeeze as much moisture as possible from the grated zucchini by twisting it, a handful at a time, in a kitchen towel or a length of cheesecloth. Sift the flour with the cornstarch, baking powder, and the 1 teaspoon salt. Put the butter in the bowl of an electric mixer and beat it with the paddle attachment on medium speed until it is very light and creamy. With the machine running, add the eggs, one at a time, adding some of the flour mixture after each egg. Beat in the remaining flour and stir in the sugar and zucchini by hand. Pour the batter into a buttered, 9 x 9-inch glass baking dish and bake for 45 minutes or until the top is golden and the center of the gratin is springy to the touch. Mix the sour cream with the lime juice, cumin, and salt and pepper to taste. Spread this mixture evenly over the gratin, sprinkle the pine nuts over the top, and return the gratin to the oven for 5 minutes more or until the sour cream begins to set.

MAKES 6 TO 8 SERVINGS

Dooryard Fruit

Key West is not an ideal place for a vegetable garden. It's too hot, except in winter, which is the only time it's possible to grow herbs. It is, however, the ideal place for dooryard fruits, which are used to season many of Shook's recipes. So named because they are fruits that grow in people's yards just outside their doors, these are varieties of produce generally unavailable in supermarkets elsewhere, and scarce even in the grocery stores of Key West.

Unlike ordinary oranges, which come off trees grown from grafted roots, sour oranges grow on trees that began as orange seeds. Every tree is an individual and produces different flavored fruit. While the sour orange is ugly and too tart to eat out of hand, it adds to recipes a flavor that no ordinary orange could deliver. At Louie's, sour oranges from people's back yard trees are used to make tart, fruity marinades for chicken and pork.

The most famous dooryard fruit is the Key lime, which is virtually impossible to buy commercially. Small, yellow, and with a vivid flavor very different from the more familiar Persian lime, the Key lime is not commercially grown but can be found in small groves of trees in private back yards. Doug Shook tells of a woman named Doris who knows where those trees are. She buys the Key limes, squeezes them, and sells the juice to Louie's kitchen. "We are one of the few places in town that

has real Key lime juice in our Key lime pie," Doug Shook says. "We also use it in sauces and to make ceviche."

One of the most distinctive dooryard fruits is the calamondin, which is extremely rare. The calamondin looks like a miniature tangerine with leathery skin. It is easy to segment and has an intense sour flavor. "You can interchange it with the Key lime," Doug Shook notes. "We use it to make mustard, and there is nothing better in a vodka tonic."

Mangos grow in abundance on Key West, and while not as uncommon as some of the other dooryard fruits, they are a beautiful symbol of the island's unique flavors. The difference between those found on supermarket shelves and the ones you eat in Key West is like the difference between a flavorless tomato and one picked fresh off a garden vine. Doug Shook sums up the magic: "There is nothing like hearing a mango bang off a tree onto your tin roof at night . . . then going out the next morning to pick it up and have it for breakfast."

MAIN DISHES

Fish Fumet

Crumb-Crusted Yellowtail

Grilled Cobia

Grilled Grouper

Montpellier Butter

Grilled Tuna

Ginger Butter Sauce

Grilled Yellowfin Tuna

Asian BBQ Sauce

Grouper in Saffron Broth

Grilled Marinated Tuna Steaks

Seared, Spice-Rubbed Tuna

Gulf Shrimp

Lobster Braised in Truffle Butter

Grilled Florida Lobster

Pan-Roasted Florida Lobster

Thai-Marinated Shrimp

Horseradish-Crusted Snapper

Annatto-Rubbed Grouper

Curried Chicken Hash

Jamaican Jerk-Rubbed Chicken Breasts

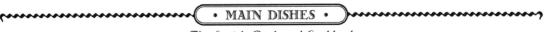
FISH FUMET

Grouper heads and skeletons make wonderful fish broth. If groupers are not available, snapper bones or those of any other light, non-oily fish can be used.

1	grouper carcass, gills removed, soaked well in cold water
1	leek (white and pale green part only), cut into 1-inch pieces
2	medium carrots, peeled and cut into 1-inch pieces
3	ribs celery with leaves, cut into 1-inch pieces
1	yellow onion, peeled and cut into 1-inch pieces
4	large mushrooms, sliced
1	medium red tomato, quartered
	Pinch of saffron threads
4	sprigs fresh thyme
4	sprigs parsley
1	bay leaf
2	teaspoons fennel seed
1	tablespoon black peppercorns
1	cup dry white wine
1	gallon water

Put the fish carcass in a large deep pot with the leek, carrots, celery, onion, mushrooms, tomato, saffron, thyme, parsley, bay leaf, fennel, and peppercorns. Cover the pot and cook over medium-high heat, stirring occasionally, for 20 minutes or until the vegetables have begun to soften and all of the contents of the pot are steamy and aromatic. Add the wine to the pot and reduce it by half. Add the water to the pot, bring to a boil, and reduce the heat to a simmer. Cook at a gentle simmer for 30 minutes. Strain the liquid, discarding the solids. Cool the fumet and store in the refrigerator for up to 3 days.

MAKES ABOUT 4 QUARTS

CRUMB-CRUSTED YELLOWTAIL
with Citrus Butter and Pickled Red Onions

Our customers love yellowtail snapper no matter how we prepare it, but this is a favorite. Other delicate, flaky fish can be served this way as well. Japanese bread crumbs are particularly light and flaky and make a distinctive crust.

PICKLED RED ONIONS:

2	quarts water
2	medium red onions (about 1 pound)
¾	cup sour orange juice or rice wine vinegar
1	teaspoon sea salt
½	teaspoon dried oregano
2	jalapeños, seeded and cut in fine julienne

FOR THE CITRUS BUTTER:

½	cup fresh orange juice
2	tablespoons fresh lime juice
2	tablespoons fresh lemon juice
½	cup chopped shallots
1	sprig fresh thyme
1	teaspoon whole black peppercorns
2	tablespoons cream
1½	cups cold, unsalted butter, cut into ½-inch cubes

6	(6-ounce) yellowtail fillets
6	tablespoons Aïoli (page 100)
2	cups Japanese breadcrumbs (panko)
4	tablespoons clarified butter

Make the pickle onions first. Bring the water to a boil in a deep pot. Peel the onions and slice them into ¼-inch rings. Drop the onions into the boiling water, stir once, and immediately drain them in a colander. Transfer the onions to a small bowl and add the orange juice, salt, oregano, and peppers. Stir well, cover and set aside for at least an hour. The onions will keep in the refrigerator for about 2 weeks.

To make the citrus butter, put the orange, lemon, and lime juices in a small, non-reactive saucepan with the shallots, thyme, and peppercorns. Place the pot over medium-high heat and cook until the juices have nearly evaporated. Add the cream to the pan, stir, and cook for 2 or 3 minutes longer. Add the butter, a few pieces at a time, stirring constantly so that each addition slowly liquefies before the next is added. When all of the butter has been incorporated, strain the sauce through a medium-mesh sieve into a small bowl and keep it warm.

To prepare the fish, spread 1 tablespoon aïoli evenly over the inside surface of each yellowtail fillet. Put the bread crumbs on a plate and press each fillet, aïoli side down, into them. Place the fillets on a plate, crumb side up. Heat 2 tablespoons of clarified butter in each of two wide skillets over medium-high heat. When the butter is hot, carefully lay the fillets in the pans, crumb side down, not overlapping, and let them cook undisturbed for 5 minutes. Turn the heat down if the breadcrumbs seem to be darkening too quickly. When the crumb crust is a nice golden color, carefully turn the fillets over with a spatula. Continue cooking the yellowtail fillets for 5 minutes longer, until the flesh at the thickest part flakes easily with the tip of a knife. Divide the citrus butter sauce among 6 large dinner plates and center a yellowtail fillet on each. Top the fish with the pickled onions and serve.

MAKES 6 SERVINGS

GRILLED COBIA
with Lemon Butter, Spaetzle, and Tomatoes

Try this also with salmon fillets, dolphin, or even tuna.

SPAETZLE:

4	*extra large egg yolks*
1	*cup milk*
1	*teaspoon sea salt*
½	*teaspoon ground black pepper*
2	*cups all-purpose flour*
1	*tablespoon olive oil*

LEMON BUTTER:

2	*fresh shallots, peeled and chopped*
1	*sprig fresh thyme*
1	*teaspoon whole black peppercorns*
1	*small bay leaf*
½	*cup fresh lemon juice*
1½	*cups unsalted butter, cut into ½-inch pieces*

2¼	*pounds cobia fillets, skin removed, cut on the bias into 6 equal pieces*
¼	*cup olive oil*
2	*tablespoons clarified butter*

2	*red ripe tomatoes, peeled, seeded, and diced*
1	*bunch fresh chives, finely snipped*

To make the spaetzle, combine the egg yolks and milk in a mixing bowl and beat well. Add the salt and pepper and mix again. Stir in the flour, adding up to ½ cup additional, if necessary, to make a stiff batter that pulls away from the sides of the bowl. Bring a large pot of salted water to a boil over high heat. Position a colander or perforated pan with holes ½ inch in diameter over the boiling water and, using a rubber spatula, push the spaetzle batter through the holes into the water. Work with about ½ cup spaetzle batter at a time. When the little dumplings float to the top of the pot, remove them with a skimmer or slotted spoon and drop them in a bowl of ice water. Repeat with the remaining spaetzle batter. When all the spaetzle has been cooked, drain it, toss it with the olive oil, and refrigerate it.

To make the lemon butter sauce, combine the shallots, thyme, peppercorns, bay leaf, and lemon juice in a small saucepan and cook over high heat until the lemon juice is nearly evaporated. Reduce the heat to medium and whisk in the butter, a few pieces at a time, allowing each addition of butter to liquefy before adding the next. When all of the butter has been added, strain the sauce through a medium-mesh sieve and keep warm.

To cook the cobia, heat a gas or charcoal grill to very hot. Brush the cobia with the cup olive oil and place on the grill skin side up. Cook for 3 minutes and gently give the cobia a quarter turn. Cook 3 minutes longer and turn the cobia over. Cook for 5 minutes on the second side, until the fish just begins to flake but is still slightly translucent at the center. While the cobia is grilling, heat the clarified butter in a wide skillet and when it is hot, add the spaetzle. Cook over high heat until browned on the bottom and then stir the spaetzle and let it brown again. It should be unevenly golden brown, some parts crisp and some pale and soft. Season the spaetzle with salt and pepper and divide it among 6 large plates, making a mound in the center of each plate. Place a piece of cobia on each mound of spaetzle. Drizzle the lemon butter sauce over the fish and around the spaetzle. Top the fish with the diced tomatoes and chives and serve.

MAKES 6 SERVINGS

Local Fish

Many people come to the Florida Keys to catch fish. Surrounded by the deep blue sea, Key West is an ideal place to eat it.

Beyond the conch that is emblematic of the island, shellfish is vastly important to Key West. The shrimp industry in particular has been a significant part of the economy for decades; and while it is no longer as important as it once was, shrimping is still big business and shrimp boats remain a presence in local waters. "Once you have had fresh Gulf shrimp, you cannot imagine eating frozen shrimp ever again," Doug Shook proclaims. Known as *pink gold*, the flavorful shrimp harvested in Gulf

Florida Fish & Wildlife Conservation Commission

Spiny Lobster

waters have a snapping marine sweetness that defines what good shrimp should be; and virtually every menu in town features them.

Spiny lobsters are another local enthusiasm. Known here also as crawfish and quite unlike North Atlantic lobsters, they are clawless critters that locals and visitors just love to eat. "As they are, they can have a kind of skunky taste," Doug Shook laughs, "but we have ways of making them succulent." Lobster season runs from early August through March.

Cobia

Stone crabs are big on Key West, too—from October 15 to May 15. The beautiful hard-shelled, pink-and-black claws (which are taken from crabs that get thrown back in the water to grow more claws) are generally served simply, on a plate with mustard sauce. But at Louie's, they are one of the three favorite regional crustaceans—along with shrimp and lobster—that go into the Chilled Buttermilk Soup (page 81).

Yellowtail snapper is probably the most popular fish on Louie's menu (and on the menu of many local restaurants). It is abundant in Key West waters and is one of the best selling meals on the island. "I enjoy eating it myself," Doug Shook says. "But sometimes we get tired of cooking it. Delicious as it is, when you cook it every day, it gets a little boring." Doug is more excited by the kinds of fish he gets in from charter boats—varieties generally unavailable from an ordinary fish supplier. "When you see wahoo or cobia on a menu, you know that they are

fresh," he notes. "Those are fish you get only from a fisherman, someone who caught them that day. The charter boat men know to call me when they have something I would like to cook."

Wahoo

GRILLED GROUPER
with Herbed Arborio Rice,
Heirloom Tomatoes, and Smoky Bacon

The day the first box of Heirloom Tomatoes arrived at Louie's Backyard was a red-letter day. We've always taken care to buy vine-ripened tomatoes and coddle them to bring out their best, refusing to serve those pale, imitation supermarket tomatoes. But that first box of heirlooms, with their striking colors and plump, nearly bursting skins, was a quantum leap in the pleasure tomatoes can bring. This is the first dish we prepared with them.

Have the Montpellier Butter and Sweet Smoky Bacon ready before beginning this recipe.

3	heirloom tomatoes, preferably 3 different varieties	2	quarts water
2	tablespoons finely chopped fresh shallots	2	cups arborio rice
		6	(6-ounce) grouper steaks, cut 1-inch thick
2	tablespoons red wine vinegar	3	tablespoons canola oil
6	tablespoons extra virgin olive oil	6	strips smoky bacon
2	teaspoons plus a pinch salt	1	cup Montpellier Butter (page 141)
	Pepper		

Heat a gas or charcoal grill to very hot. Wash the tomatoes, remove the cores, and, with an exceptionally sharp knife, gently cut them into 1-inch pieces. Carefully place the tomato pieces, with their skins and seeds intact, in a small bowl. In another bowl whisk together the shallots, vinegar, olive oil, and salt. Season the vinaigrette with pepper to taste. Bring the water to a boil, add a pinch of salt and the rice, and cook over high heat for 9 to 11 minutes or until the rice is just cooked through. Drain the rice in a colander and keep warm. While the rice is cooking, brush the grouper with the oil and season well with salt and pepper to taste. Place the steaks on the grill and cook for 2 minutes. Give the steaks a quarter turn and cook for 2 or 3 minutes longer; then turn them over and cook on the second side for 5 to 6 minutes more. The grouper should be just cooked through, hot but still translucent in the center and yielding to large flakes when pressed with a finger. Remove the grouper from the grill. Briefly cook the bacon slices on the grill to warm and crisp them. Take them off the grill and cut into ¼-inch pieces. Toss the hot rice in a bowl with the Montpellier Butter

to coat each grain. Divide the rice among six large dinner plates, flattening it out with the back of a spoon to cover the service area of the plate. Center a grouper steak on each plate. Very gently combine the tomatoes with the vinaigrette. Divide the tomatoes among the plates, placing them right on top of the grouper. Julienne the bacon and top the tomatoes with the bacon to serve.

MAKES 6 SERVINGS

MONTPELLIER BUTTER

This will keep for at least 2 weeks in the refrigerator, although it has so many uses it's not likely to last that long. Try it on grilled fish or sirloin, on any green vegetable, or tossed into pasta.

1	cup fresh spinach leaves, stems removed	4	tablespoons capers
1	cup watercress, leaves and tender stems only	2	cloves garlic
		1	teaspoon sea salt
4	tablespoons chopped Italian parsley	½	teaspoon freshly ground black pepper
4	tablespoons chopped chervil	½	teaspoon cayenne
4	tablespoons chopped chives	6	hard-cooked extra large egg yolks
2	tablespoons chopped tarragon	4	extra large egg yolks
½	cup chopped shallots	½	pound unsalted butter
4	cornichons	1	cup extra virgin olive oil
8	oil-packed anchovies	1	tablespoon white wine vinegar

Bring a large pot of salted water to a boil, add the spinach and watercress leaves, stir, and immediately drain in a colander. Rinse the greens under cool running water and drain again, gently squeezing out as much water as possible. In the work bowl of a food processor, combine the blanched greens with the parsley, chervil, chives, tarragon, shallots, cornichons, anchovies, capers, garlic, salt, pepper, and cayenne. Process to finely chop everything; then add the egg yolks and process to combine well. Add the butter and, with the machine running, slowly add the oil and vinegar. Transfer the butter to a clean container and store in the refrigerator.

MAKES ABOUT 4 CUPS

GRILLED TUNA
with Ginger Butter Sauce, Roasted Shiitakes, and Sweet and Sour Tomatoes

Fermented black beans are soy beans that are salted and cured with ginger. They are available at Oriental markets. They're used like capers in this dish, providing little surprising bites of their strong flavor.

1½	cups Ginger Butter Sauce (page 143)
½	cup Sweet and Sour Tomatoes (page 108)
18	large shiitake mushroom caps
2	teaspoons chopped fresh garlic
1	tablespoon roasted sesame oil
3	plus 3 tablespoons canola oil
	Sea salt
	Freshly ground black pepper
6	(6-ounce) tuna steaks cut 1-inch thick
18	large asparagus spears, steamed
4½	cups cooked white basmati rice
2	tablespoons fermented black beans

Make the Ginger Butter Sauce and the Sweet and Sour Tomatoes before beginning to grill the tuna.

For the roasted shiitakes, preheat the oven to 400°F. Toss the mushroom caps with the garlic, sesame oil, 3 tablespoons of the canola oil, and salt and pepper to taste in a small bowl. Transfer the mushrooms to a shallow baking dish, cover with foil, and place in the oven for 20 minutes. The mushroom caps should be hot, fragrant, and yielding to gentle pressure from your finger. Keep the mushrooms covered in a warm place while the tuna is grilling.

To grill the tuna, heat a charcoal or gas grill to very hot. Brush the tuna steaks all over with the remaining 3 tablespoons of canola oil and place them on the grill. Cook for 2 minutes; then give the steaks a quarter turn and cook for 2 minutes more. Turn the tuna steaks over and cook for 2 minutes more. The tuna should still be quite rare on the inside. Remove the tuna from the grill. Briefly cook the asparagus spears on the

grill just to mark them and warm them through. Divide the rice and asparagus among six large dinner plates. Ladle 2 ounces of the Ginger Butter Sauce onto each plate and center a tuna steak in the pool of sauce. Spoon 1 tablespoon of the Sweet and Sour Tomatoes onto each tuna steak, place the mushroom caps around the tuna, and scatter the fermented black beans over everything.

MAKES 6 SERVINGS

GINGER BUTTER SAUCE

This sauce can be served with nearly any grilled or sautéed fish, and is also excellent with sautéed sweetbreads.

4	tablespoons fresh ginger, peeled and coarsely chopped
2	teaspoons fresh garlic, peeled and chopped
4	tablespoons fresh shallots, peeled and chopped
½	cup sherry

1	tablespoon sherry vinegar
1	tablespoon sweet-hot mustard (like Honeycup or Dijon)
2	tablespoons cream (optional)
1	pound unsalted butter, cold, cut into ½-inch cubes

In a small saucepan, combine the ginger, garlic, shallots, sherry, sherry vinegar, and mustard. Cook over medium-high heat until the liquid has almost completely evaporated. Add the cream if using and cook again until the cream has reduced by half. Add the butter a few pieces at a time, stirring constantly with a wire whisk or a wooden spoon; keep the pan over medium heat. As the butter liquefies, add more until all of it has been incorporated into a smooth, creamy sauce. Be careful not to let the sauce get too hot or the butter, instead of liquefying, will melt and separate. Strain the sauce through a medium sieve, discard the solids, and keep the sauce warm over a pan of hot water. The cream helps to stabilize the sauce and makes it a little easier to keep the emulsion of butter fat, milk solids, and water intact, but the sauce can be made successfully without it.

MAKES 2 CUPS

GRILLED YELLOWFIN TUNA
with Papaya, Sweet Soy, and Wakame Salad

This dish has a lot of parts, but none of them are difficult or time-consuming, and their combined effect is stunning to the eye and the palate. Bottled Japanese Katsu sauce (found in Asian markets) can be substituted for the Asian BBQ. Prepare all of the sauces and garnishes before starting to cook the tuna.

WAKAME SALAD:

1½	cups frozen wakame salad (available at Japanese specialty stores)
1	cup European cucumber, peeled, seeded, and finely diced

SERVING SAUCE:

½	cup soy sauce
½	cup Sweet Soy Sauce (page 101)
½	cup mirin
6	(6-ounce) tuna steaks cut 1-inch thick
3	tablespoons canola oil
2	cups Asian Barbecue Sauce (page 145)
4½	cups cooked sticky rice
1	ripe papaya, peeled, seeded, and cut into 12 lengthwise slices
2	cups Spicy Mayonnaise (page 110)
2	teaspoons black sesame seeds
4	tablespoons wasabi powder mixed with enough cool water to make a stiff paste

To make the Wakame salad, toss the thawed seaweed mixture with the diced cucumber. Keep cold. To make the serving sauce, stir together the soy sauce, Sweet Soy Sauce, and mirin and set aside.

Heat a charcoal or gas grill to very hot. When the grill is ready, brush the tuna steaks with the canola oil and place them on the grill. Grill the tuna for 2 minutes and turn the steaks by 90 degrees. Grill for 2 minutes more and turn the steaks over. Brush the steaks liberally with the barbecue sauce and continue grilling for 2 minutes longer. The tuna should be still quite rare in the center. Remove the tuna steaks from the heat, brush again with the barbecue sauce, and set aside.

On each of six large dinner plates put three small balls of sticky rice and 2 ounces of the serving sauce. Place 2 slices of papaya and a tuna steak in the center of the sauce. Drizzle the spicy mayonnaise over the tuna. Place a spoonful of the wakame salad over one corner of each tuna steak, sprinkle the plates with the sesame seeds, and garnish each with 1 tablespoon of the wasabi paste in a little mound on the plate's rim.

MAKES 6 SERVINGS

ASIAN BARBECUE SAUCE

We use this sauce primarily for grilled tuna, but it works as well on other fish, pork and chicken. We also serve it drizzled over fried vegetable spring rolls.

½	cup soy sauce
½	cup Sweet Soy Sauce (page 101)
½	cup molasses
½	cup ketchup
4	tablespoons fermented black beans

Combine the soy sauce, Sweet Soy Sauce, molasses, ketchup, and black beans in a blender and blend until smooth.

MAKES 2 CUPS

GROUPER IN SAFFRON BROTH
with Mussels, Leeks, and Potatoes

Any firm-fleshed white fish can be substituted for the grouper. Cod would be particularly suitable.

2	large Idaho potatoes, peeled and cut julienne with a mandoline		Sea salt
			Freshly ground black pepper
2	plus 1 tablespoons canola oil	5	cups Fish Fumet
3	large leeks (white and pale green parts only), trimmed, washed, and cut julienne	1	teaspoon saffron threads
		36	mussels, beards trimmed and washed
6	(6-ounce) grouper fillets, cut about 1-inch thick	1	plus ½ cup Aïoli (page 100)
		2	tablespoons chopped Italian parsley

Blanch the potatoes in boiling salted water for 3 minutes. Drain well. In a large, deep pot or Dutch oven, heat 2 tablespoons of the canola oil and stir in the leeks. When the leeks have softened, add the potatoes to the pan; stir to combine them with the leeks and set the pan off the heat. Season the grouper fillets with salt and pepper. Heat 1 tablespoon of the canola oil in a wide skillet; when it is nearly smoking, add 3 of the grouper fillets to the pan. Cook the fish on one side for 2 or 3 minutes or until nicely browned. Turn the fish over and brown the other side. Remove the fish from the skillet and lay them on top of the leeks and potatoes in the deep pot. Repeat with the remaining fish. Add the fish fumet and saffron to the pot, place over medium heat, and bring to a simmer. Add the mussels to the pot, cover, and cook for 8 to 10 minutes longer or until the mussels have opened and the fish are just cooked through, still translucent at the center but yielding to gentle pressure. Carefully divide the fish, mussels, and vegetables among six wide soup plates, leaving the broth behind. Put 1 cup of the aïoli in a small bowl and whisk 1 cup of the hot broth into it to temper it. Whisk this mixture back into the remaining broth and place over low heat. Cook, stirring constantly, for 1 minute longer, until very hot and slightly thickened. Do not let the mixture boil. Ladle the aïoli-enriched saffron broth over the fish and vegetables in each bowl. Place a generous tablespoon of aïoli in the center of each bowl and sprinkle with the chopped parsley.

MAKES 6 GENEROUS SERVINGS

Bob Elkins, Fisherman

Bob Elkins does not work at Louie's Backyard, but he makes a vital contribution to the menu: fresh grouper. In the mornings, he goes far out into the Atlantic, dives in, and, using a speargun, bags some three hundred pounds of fish, which he immediately brings to the restaurant. As Doug Shook describes it, "He fights the sharks to get his catch. Sometimes when I am cutting them up, I'm cutting around the shark bites.

"It's exciting to cut fish so fresh," Doug says. "As you run the knife through to cut fillets, you feel it still quivering under your hand."

One day at Louie's we met Bob Elkins as he brought some local grouper into the kitchen. We watched Doug Shook cut up the fish moments later. He rubbed the fillets with annatto and grilled them and served them with black beans and mango salsa . . . within only a few hours of their swimming in the ocean waters.

GRILLED, MARINATED TUNA STEAKS
with Indian River Grapefruit and Red Onion Compote

With the shrinking global market and the improvements in shipping, it seems that nearly any fruit or vegetable can be found at any given time of the year. In the tropics we seem even further out of touch with the seasonal rhythms that tell us when to eat peas or strawberries or late summer corn. But grapefruit . . . we know it's winter when the grapefruit is great. An Indian River grapefruit in February or March, particularly when there's been some seriously cold weather on the Florida peninsula, is what they mean when they say "Fresh Fruit in Season": firm and glowing and pumped full of itself.

MARINADE:

3	cloves garlic, peeled and chopped
2	teaspoons sea salt
1	cup chopped fresh cilantro
1	teaspoon freshly ground black pepper
¾	cup olive oil
½	cup dry white wine
4	tablespoons fresh lemon juice
6	(6-ounce) tuna steaks, cut 1-inch thick

GRAPEFRUIT AND RED ONION COMPOTE:

3	ruby red Indian River grapefruit
2	tablespoons unsalted butter
2	tablespoons olive oil
3	red onions, about 1½ pounds, peeled and sliced lengthwise into ¼-inch slices
	Sea salt
	Freshly ground black pepper

For the marinade, combine the garlic, salt, cilantro, pepper, olive oil, wine, and lemon juice in a blender and blend to a smooth purée. Lay the tuna steaks in a glass dish large enough to hold them in one layer and pour the marinade over them. Turn the tuna over in the marinade to coat it well. Cover the dish and refrigerate for at least 4 hours, preferably overnight.

To prepare the grapefruit and onion mix, begin by slicing off the stem and blossom ends of the grapefruit, exposing the pulp. With a sharp paring knife, cut away the rind, including all the white pith and the outer membrane of the grapefruit sections. Cut the grapefruit flesh into sections, peeling it away from the surrounding membrane

with the paring knife. Discard the seeds. Place the grapefruit sections in a small bowl and set aside. Squeeze the juice from the membrane and from the ends of the fruit into another small bowl. Heat the butter and olive oil in a wide, deep pot with a lid over medium-high heat. Add the sliced onions and stir well to coat them with the butter and oil. Cook for 2 or 3 minutes over medium-high heat until they begin to soften; then cover the pan, turn the heat to very low, and cook the onions for 30 minutes longer, stirring occasionally until they are very soft, sweet, and tender. They shouldn't take on any color at all. After 30 minutes, remove the lid, turn the heat up to medium, and add the reserved grapefruit juice to the pan. Cook, stirring often, until nearly all of the liquid has evaporated and the onions have become a thick jam. Transfer the onions to a bowl and set them aside to cool. When the onions have cooled to room temperature, season them to taste with sea salt and black pepper and gently fold in the grapefruit sections.

To cook the tuna, heat a gas or charcoal grill to very hot. Lay the tuna steaks on the grill and cook for 2 minutes. Give the steaks a quarter turn and cook for 2 minutes longer. Turn the steaks over and cook for 3 to 4 minutes on the second side. The tuna should still be rare in the center. Top each tuna steak with a generous spoonful of the Grapefruit and Red Onion Compote and serve.

MAKES 6 SERVINGS

SEARED SPICE-RUBBED TUNA
with Spinach, Watercress, and Red Grapes

Increasing the portions of tuna would make this a great summer supper out on the deck by the pool.

½	teaspoon Boyajian Orange Oil (see note)
2	tablespoons canola oil
1¼	pounds sushi-grade yellowfin tuna, about 10 x 2 x 2 inches

SPICE RUB:

2	tablespoons whole black peppercorns
2	tablespoons coriander seed
2	tablespoons anise seed
1	tablespoon kosher salt

DRESSING:

2	tablespoons fresh orange juice
1	tablespoon balsamic vinegar
1½	teaspoons red wine vinegar
2	teaspoons honey
1	teaspoon chopped garlic
6	tablespoons extra virgin olive oil
2	tablespoons hot water
½	teaspoon sea salt

SHALLOT GARNISH:

3	large fresh shallots, peeled and sliced into ⅛-inch thick rings
½	cup flour
1	tablespoon reserved spice rub
2	cups canola oil for frying

SALAD:

3	cups watercress, stems removed, washed and dried
3	cups tender spinach, stems removed, washed and dried
1½	cups seedless red grapes, rinsed, cut in half

Combine the orange and canola oils and brush the mixture over all surfaces of the tuna. For the spice rub, grind the peppercorns, coriander, anise, and salt in a spice grinder. Set 1 tablespoon of the spice rub aside for the shallot garnish. Coat the tuna with the spice rub. Heat a large cast-iron skillet over high heat until it is smoking hot. Place the tuna in the pan and sear it for 45 seconds on each side. The tuna will be essentially raw under the crust of seared spices. Refrigerate the tuna.

For the dressing, combine the orange juice, vinegars, honey, garlic, and olive oil in the jar of a blender. Turn on the blender and slowly add the water. Season with the salt.

Make the shallot garnish by tossing the shallot rings in the flour and reserved spice rub. Drop them into the oil, heated to 375°F, and fry them until they are brown and crisp. Drain the shallots on paper towels.

To serve, slice the tuna into very thin slices and arrange them in a spoke-like fashion on individual plates. Toss the watercress, spinach, and grapes in a bowl with the salad dressing and mound them in the center of each plate. Drizzle any dressing remaining in the bowl over the tuna. Garnish the greens with the fried shallot rings and serve.

MAKE 6 SERVINGS

Note: You may use 2 teaspoons grated orange zest if you can't find the orange oil.

GULF SHRIMP
with Bacon, Mushrooms, and Stone-Ground Grits

A casual conversation about shrimp in a bar led to this low-country preparation, which has proved to be among the most popular shrimp dishes that have appeared on the menu.

2	tablespoons clarified butter
2	cups quartered button mushroom caps
36	jumbo pink Gulf shrimp (about 2 pounds) peeled and deveined
2	cups diced slab bacon, cooked and drained
¼	cup fresh lemon juice
¼	cup chopped Italian parsley
½	pound unsalted butter at room temperature
	Stone-Ground Grits with Cheddar (page 123)
	Lemon wedges for garnish

Heat the clarified butter in a very large skillet or two smaller ones. When it is nearly smoking, add the mushrooms. Cook for 3 or 4 minutes, stirring, until the mushrooms have begun to brown on the edges. Add the shrimp and cook for 2 or 3 minutes longer or until the shrimp have turned bright pink and begun to curl. Stir in the bacon, lemon juice, and parsley and bring to a boil. Add the unsalted butter and shake or stir to keep everything moving while the butter liquefies into a sauce that coats the shrimp. Divide the grits among six deep plates and spoon the shrimp mixture over them. Garnish with the lemon wedges.

MAKES 6 SERVINGS

LOBSTER BRAISED IN TRUFFLE BUTTER
with Spinach and Prosciutto

This recipe has been requested more than any other we've served at Louie's Backyard. It's a fixture on the menu during lobster season, which runs from August through March.

TRUFFLE BUTTER:

½   cup chopped shallots

1   cup sautérne or other sweet white wine

4   tablespoons unsalted butter at room temperature

2   tablespoons Italian white truffle oil

2   (6-ounce) spiny lobster tails

1   cup heavy cream

4   ounces julienned prosciutto

2   cups baby spinach, stems removed, washed

   Sea salt

   Freshly ground black pepper

For the truffle butter, place the shallots and wine in a small, nonreactive saucepan and cook over medium heat until most of the wine has evaporated. Remove from the heat, transfer to a mixing bowl, and allow to cool. When the shallots are cool, beat in the butter and the truffle oil.

To prepare the lobster, wrap each lobster tail tightly in several layers of plastic wrap. Bring a large pot of water to a boil. (Use about 3 cups water per 6-ounce lobster tail.) Add the wrapped lobster tails and cook for exactly 6 minutes. Remove the lobster tails with tongs or a slotted spoon and transfer them to a bowl of ice water. When the lobster tails have cooled, drain them and remove the plastic wrap. Place one lobster tail on a cutting board, spiny side down and split it in half, cutting directly through the shell with a sharp, sturdy knife. Remove the intestinal vein from each half of the lobster tail and pull the meat out of the shell. The lobster will not be fully cooked at this point. Repeat with the remaining lobster tails.

When ready to serve, place the heavy cream in a wide saucepan or deep skillet and bring to a simmer. Add the lobster and prosciutto and cook until the cream is reduced by half. Add the spinach, cooking until the spinach is wilted and the sauce is thick and glossy. Season with salt and pepper and add the truffle butter. Stir the butter quickly into the sauce so the fat does not separate. Divide the mixture among four small bowls or deep plates. Serve at once.

MAKE 4 SERVINGS

GRILLED FLORIDA LOBSTER
with Swiss Chard, Mango, and Chardonnay Butter

This dish hits all the notes, from the earthy hint of beets in the Swiss chard to the elusive hint of vanilla in the Chardonnay butter.

6	*(6- to 7-ounce) Florida lobster tails in the shell*
3	*tablespoons clarified butter*

SWISS CHARD:

2	*bunches Swiss chard, preferably Bright Lights (about 2 pounds)*
1	*lemon*
1	*large mango, ripe but firm, peeled and cut into ½-inch cubes*

CHARDONNAY BUTTER:

½	*cup finely chopped fresh shallots*
1	*small bay leaf*
1	*(2-inch) piece vanilla bean, split*
1½	*cups Chardonnay*
2	*tablespoons cream*
1½	*cups cold unsalted butter, cut into ½-inch cubes*
	Sea salt
	Freshly ground pepper

To prepare the lobster tails, wrap each one tightly in several layers of plastic wrap. Bring a large pot of water to a boil. (Use about 3 cups water per 6-ounce lobster tail.) Add the wrapped lobster tails and cook for exactly 6 minutes. Remove the lobster tails with tongs or a slotted spoon and transfer them to a bowl of ice water. When the lobster tails have cooled, drain them and remove the plastic wrap. Place one lobster tail on a cutting board, spiny side down and split it in half, cutting directly through the shell with sharp, sturdy knife. Remove the intestinal vein from each half of the lobster tail and pull the meat out of the shell. The lobster will not be fully cooked at this point. Repeat with the remaining lobster tails.

To prepare the Swiss chard, strip the leaves from the stems, wash them well, and tear them into 2- to 3-inch pieces. Discard the stems or reserve them for another use.

Remove the zest from the lemon with a citrus zester. Combine the cubed mango, zest, and juice from the lemon in a small bowl.

To make the Chardonnay butter, place the shallots, bay leaf, and vanilla bean in a small, nonreactive saucepan with the Chardonnay. Place the pan over medium-high heat and cook until the wine has nearly evaporated. Add the cream to the pan and continue cooking for another minute or two. Add the butter, a few pieces at a time, stirring constantly so that each addition slowly liquefies before the next is added. When all of the butter has been incorporated, strain the sauce through a medium-mesh sieve into a small bowl. Season it to taste with salt and pepper, and keep it warm.

Bring a large pot of salted water to a boil. Heat the clarified butter in a wide skillet and when it is hot, add the lobster, shell side down. Cook the pieces of lobster for 3 or 4 minutes, season them with salt and pepper, and turn them over. Continue cooking for 4 or 5 minutes longer or until the lobster is just barely opaque at the thickest part. While the lobster is cooking, add the Swiss chard to the boiling water, stir well, and immediately drain in a colander. Transfer the chard to a bowl and toss it with half of the Chardonnay butter before mounding it in the center of a serving platter or individual plates. Arrange the lobster over the Swiss chard and drizzle the remaining chardonnay butter over the lobster and around the chard on the plate. Top the lobster with the mango-lemon mixture and serve.

MAKES 6 SERVINGS

PAN-ROASTED FLORIDA LOBSTER
with Spinach Pasta, Tomatoes, and Tomato Butter

August, when Florida lobster season opens, is also a good time for tomatoes, and this recipe makes the most of both. The lobster could also be grilled; follow the same procedure for precooking the lobster tails. Split them in half and grill them in their shells.

6	*(5- to 6-ounce) Florida lobster tails in the shell*		**TOMATO GARNISH:**	
			1	*pound ripe tomatoes, a mixture of yellow and red if possible*
TOMATOES AND TOMATO BUTTER:				
12	*red ripe plum tomatoes*		12	*cherry tomatoes*
4	*tablespoons red wine vinegar*		12	*large fresh basil leaves*
2	*tablespoons cream*			
1½	*cups cold, unsalted butter, cut into ½-inch pieces*		12	*ounces spinach fettuccine*
			2	*cups fine dry breadcrumbs*
	Sea salt		4	*tablespoons clarified butter*
	Freshly ground black pepper			

To prepare the lobster tails, wrap each one tightly in several layers of plastic wrap. Bring a large pot of water to a boil. (Use about 3 cups water per 6-ounce lobster tail.) Add the wrapped lobster tails and cook for exactly 6 minutes. Remove the lobster tails with tongs or a slotted spoon and transfer them to a bowl of ice water. When the lobster tails have cooled, drain them and remove the plastic wrap. Place one lobster tail on a cutting board, spiny side down and split it in half, cutting directly through the shell with sharp, sturdy knife. Remove the intestinal vein from each half of the lobster tail and pull the meat out of the shell. The lobster will not be fully cooked at this point. Repeat with the remaining lobster tails.

To make the sauce, remove the stem end from the plum tomatoes, cut them into quarters, and purée them in a food processor. Strain the purée through a medium-mesh sieve into a small saucepan. Add the red wine vinegar. Place the saucepan over medium-high heat and cook, stirring occasionally, for 10 to 12 minutes, until the purée has reduced to a thick paste that lets you glimpse the bottom of the pan when you stir it. Add the cream, stir well, and continue to cook for 3 minutes longer. Reduce the heat to medium. Add the butter, a few pieces at a time, stirring constantly so that each

addition has nearly melted before the next is added. Don't let the sauce boil. When all the butter has been added, taste the sauce and season with salt and pepper. Keep the sauce warm.

For the tomato garnish, cut the stem ends from the yellow and red tomatoes and, using a very sharp knife to avoid crushing the flesh, cut them into ½-inch cubes with the skin and seeds intact. Place them in a small bowl. Cut the cherry tomatoes into quarters and add them to the bowl. Mix the tomatoes together very gently. Make a stack of 3 or 4 basil leaves and roll it up like a cigar. With a very sharp knife, cut the roll into thin strips. Repeat with the remaining basil.

Preheat the oven to 450°F. Bring a large pot of salted water to a boil for the pasta. Remove the lobster from the refrigerator, roll each half tail in the breadcrumbs, and place them on a plate not touching each other. Heat the clarified butter in a wide skillet over medium-high heat. Add the lobster pieces to the skillet. The lobster should sizzle when it touches the hot butter. Keep the pieces of lobster at least an inch apart in the skillet. Cook them in two batches if necessary. When the breadcrumbs have become a nice golden color, after 3 minutes or so, turn the pieces over and brown the other side. Transfer the lobster to a plate lined with paper towels. Pour off any butter remaining in the skillet. Put the lobster back in the skillet in a single layer and place the skillet in the oven for 8 to 10 minutes.

While the lobster is cooking, drop the spinach fettuccine into the boiling water and cook for 4 to 8 minutes, depending on the freshness and thickness of the pasta, until it is just tender. Drain the pasta well, place it in a small bowl, and toss it with 4 tablespoons of the tomato butter.

To serve, divide the pasta among six dinner plates, mounding it in the center. Ladle the tomato butter around the pasta. Place 2 half lobster tails on top of the pasta on each plate and spoon the fresh, diced tomatoes over the lobster. Garnish with the basil chiffonade.

MAKES 6 SERVINGS

THAI-MARINATED SHRIMP
with Asian Vegetables and Spicy Peanut Sauce

The fish sauce, Chinese chili paste with garlic, and unsweetened coconut milk are becoming more readily available in good super markets. Fresh lemongrass may not be so easy to find and can be omitted without doing great harm to the recipe.

MARINADE:

4	cloves fresh garlic, peeled
2	small, hot red chiles, or ¼ teaspoon crushed red pepper
4	tablespoons Thai fish sauce (Nam Pla)
½	cup fresh lime juice
4	fresh shallots, peeled
2	tablespoons sugar
1	stalk fresh lemongrass, white and pale purple parts only, finely sliced
4	tablespoons canola oil
2	pounds Gulf shrimp, peeled and deveined

SAUCE:

2	tablespoons finely chopped fresh cilantro
1	jalapeño, stemmed and seeded
1	fresh shallot, peeled
1	tablespoon sugar
3	tablespoons fresh lime juice
1	tablespoon Thai fish sauce (Nam Pla)
¼	cup peanut butter

¾	cup unsweetened coconut milk
1	teaspoon Chinese chili paste with garlic, or to taste

VEGETABLES:

4	cups finely sliced Napa cabbage
2	cups daikon radishes, cut in julienne
1	red bell pepper, stemmed, seeded, cut in julienne
2	jalapeños, stemmed, seeded, cut in julienne
4	scallions, trimmed and sliced, white and green parts
2	small carrots, peeled and cut in julienne
1	English cucumber, cut in half, seeded, and cut into ¼-inch slices
2	plus 2 tablespoons canola oil

GARNISH:

12	cherry tomatoes, thinly sliced
6	tablespoons roasted peanuts, roughly chopped
½	cup whole fresh cilantro leaves

To make the marinade, combine the garlic, chiles, fish sauce, lime juice, shallots, sugar, lemongrass, and canola in the work bowl of a food processor or blender jar and process to a smooth paste. Toss the shrimp in a bowl with the marinade, cover, and refrigerate for at least 30 minutes or up to 2 hours.

To make the sauce, combine the cilantro, jalapeño, shallot, sugar, lime juice, fish sauce, and peanut butter in the work bowl of a food processor and purée to a smooth paste. With the machine running, slowly pour in the coconut milk. Transfer the sauce to a small bowl and add the chili paste, a little at a time, tasting as you go and stopping when it's hot enough for your taste. Prepare the cabbage, radishes, peppers, scallions, carrots, and cucumber and toss them together in a large bowl. Heat 2 tablespoons of the canola oil in a large sauté pan or wok over high heat. When the oil is nearly smoking, add the vegetable mixture. Cook, stirring and tossing, for about 3 minutes or until the vegetables are uniformly hot and have just begun to wilt. Add the peanut sauce to the pan and continue to stir and toss the vegetables until they are evenly coated with the sauce. Transfer the vegetables to a platter or individual plates, wipe out the pan, and return it to the heat. Put the remaining 2 tablespoons of canola oil in the pan. Drain the shrimp from the marinade and when the oil in the pan is very hot, add the shrimp to the pan. Stir and toss the shrimp to coat them evenly with the oil and cook for 4 to 5 minutes or until the shrimp are curled and bright pink and barely opaque at the center. Arrange the shrimp over the vegetables, scatter the sliced cherry tomatoes, chopped peanuts, and cilantro leaves over the vegetables, and serve with plain, boiled Jasmine rice.

MAKES 4 TO 6 SERVINGS

HORSERADISH-CRUSTED SNAPPER
with Roasted Garlic Vinaigrette and Fried Leeks

Sous-Chef Brendan Orr devised this preparation for the Catch of the Day section of the dinner menu, and while it appeared there, it outsold any of our other fish offerings by far. This method will work with nearly any fish fillet.

ROASTED GARLIC VINAIGRETTE:

¼	cup Roasted Garlic Cloves (page 109)
¾	teaspoon dry mustard
6	tablespoons champagne vinegar
1	cup extra virgin olive oil
½	teaspoon sea salt
½	teaspoon freshly ground black pepper
2	tablespoons snipped fresh chives
2	cups canola oil, for frying
2	large leeks, white and pale green parts, washed well, cut in julienne (about 3 inches long)

HORSERADISH CRUST:

2	tablespoons prepared horseradish
¾	teaspoon Dijon mustard
1	extra large egg yolk
½	cup canola oil
¼	cup extra virgin olive oil
1	tablespoon lemon juice
½	teaspoon sea salt
3	cups Japanese breadcrumbs
6	skinless snapper fillets, about 6 ounces each
2	plus 2 tablespoons clarified butter
1	recipe Bacon Sage Potatoes (page 119)

To make the vinaigrette, combine the garlic, mustard, and vinegar in the jar of a blender and blend to a smooth paste. Drizzle in the oil with the machine running. Transfer the vinaigrette to a small bowl, season with salt and pepper, and stir in the chives.

To fry the leeks, heat the canola oil in a small saucepan to 375°F. Add the leeks, and cook for 3 to 4 minutes, stirring until the leeks are browned and crisp. Drain the leeks on paper towels.

To make the crust, combine the horseradish, mustard, and egg yolk in the work bowl of a food processor and process to combine. With the machine running, slowly drizzle in the oils to make a thick emulsion. Add the lemon juice and salt. Lay the snapper fillets, skin side down, on a plate. Spread each one with 2 to 3 tablespoons of the horseradish mayonnaise. Reserve 6 tablespoons of the mayonnaise. Press the spread side of the fish into the Japanese breadcrumbs, using gentle pressure to make the crumbs adhere to the fish. Set the fillets on a plate, crumb side up. Heat 2 tablespoons of clarified butter in each of two medium sauté pans and when it is hot, carefully add the fillets to the pans, crumb side down. Cook the fillets over medium-high heat for 3 to 4 minutes, until the crumbs are golden brown and the fish begins to appear opaque at the edges. Carefully turn the fillets over and continue cooking for 4 minutes longer, until the fish just flakes easily when prodded with the tip of a knife.

To serve, spoon 3 to 4 tablespoons of the vinaigrette onto each of six dinner plates. Place a fillet over the vinaigrette on each plate, crumb side up. Top the fillet with a spoonful of the mayonnaise and garnish with the fried leeks. Serve the Bacon Sage Potatoes alongside the fish.

MAKES 6 SERVINGS

Southernmost

At the intersection of Whitehead and South Street, between South Beach and Fort Taylor, seventy-five miles from the Dry Tortugas, you will find the southernmost point in the continental United States. The plot of land overlooks the Atlantic Ocean and is designated by a nine-thousand-pound concrete monument resembling a black, red and yellow buoy. From dawn until long after dusk, visitors stand on this spot to have their pictures taken.

Before the heavyweight marker was installed, there was a small driftwood sign underneath the corner cork tree; actually, there were countless such signs, one after another. Souvenir-hunters kept stealing them, and so finally the immovable buoy was installed.

Along the street near the buoy, tables are set up from which tourists can buy conch shells, seashell lamps, key rings, refrigerator magnets, and other such souvenirs to commemorate their visit.

On the adjoining streets all around the point are dozens of businesses and tourist attractions that boast of being *southernmost*: the southernmost hotel, southernmost motel, southernmost guest house, southernmost private house, southernmost pharmacy, southernmost nail salon, southernmost hairdresser, and southernmost one-hour photo lab. There is even a nearby southernmost soccer club.

As a reminder of just how *far out* this southernmost point is, the concrete marker is emblazoned not with the stars and stripes or the flag of Florida, but with the emblem that signals Key West's independent spirit: a conch shell in a triangle, symbol of the not-so-mythical realm known as the Conch Republic.

ANNATTO-RUBBED GROUPER
with Black Beans and Mango Salsa

Annatto paste is a Yucatan seasoning made from the ground seeds of the annatto tree. The seeds are a deep orange color. (They're also used to give Cheddar cheese its color.)

ANNATTO RUB:

¼ cup annatto paste

¼ cup sour orange juice, or substitute mild white vinegar

½ cup olive oil

2 cloves fresh garlic, peeled and finely chopped

1 teaspoon dry oregano

2¼ pounds black grouper fillet, skin removed, cut on the bias into 6 equal pieces

MANGO SALSA:

1 large mango, ripe but still firm, peeled and diced

2 jalapeños, stemmed, seeded, and minced

½ red bell pepper, stemmed, seeded, and diced

½ small red onion, peeled and diced

1 small ripe tomato, seeded and diced

¼ cup chopped fresh cilantro

2 limes, juiced

Salt

Freshly ground pepper

4 cups cooked Black Beans (page 117)

To make the annatto rub, dissolve the paste in the orange juice in a glass or stainless bowl, mashing the annatto paste with a fork to break it up. Mix in the olive oil, garlic, and dry oregano. Pour the rub over the fish in a shallow dish and turn the grouper to coat it evenly. Refrigerate the fish for 30 to 60 minutes.

For the salsa, combine the mango, peppers, onion, tomato, cilantro, lime juice, salt, and pepper and mix them together well. Keep the salsa cold. Heat the black beans if necessary. Heat a gas or charcoal grill until it is very hot. Place the grouper on the grill, skin side up, and cook undisturbed for 5 minutes. Very carefully, slip a spatula under the fish and give each piece a quarter turn. Cook for 3 minutes longer. Carefully turn the fish over and cook for 3 or 4 minutes or until the fish will flake under gentle pressure and is nearly opaque at the center. Divide the black beans among six dinner plates, spreading them out in a circle. Center a piece of grouper on each plate, spoon some mango salsa over each piece of fish, and serve with Yellow Rice (page 127) or Fried Plantain Chips (page 123)

MAKES 6 SERVINGS

CURRIED CHICKEN HASH

This is comfort food, great by itself or topped with poached eggs. It can be prepared a day or two ahead of time up to the point of baking it, making it a great buffet dish or Christmas morning brunch.

1	*(3-pound) frying chicken*
1	*plus 1 large yellow onion, peeled and cut into 1-inch pieces*
3	*plus 3 ribs celery, trimmed and cut into 1-inch pieces*
1	*large carrot, peeled and cut into 1-inch pieces*
1	*bay leaf*
1	*sprig fresh thyme*
1	*sprig parsley*
2	*teaspoons whole black peppercorns*
4	*plus 2 tablespoons butter*
1	*red bell pepper, stemmed, seeded, and diced*
1	*green bell pepper, stemmed, seeded, and diced*
2	*Granny Smith apples, cored, peeled, and diced*
2	*tablespoons curry powder*
1	*plus ½ teaspoon sea salt*
¼	*teaspoon cayenne*
2	*cups apple juice*
2	*tablespoons all-purpose flour*
2	*cups half-and-half*
4	*tablespoons chopped Italian parsley*
4	*tablespoons sweet pickle relish*
1	*cup breadcrumbs*
2	*tablespoons butter, cut into pea-sized bits*

To poach the chicken, place it in a large, deep pot with 1 yellow onion, 3 ribs celery, the carrot, bay leaf, thyme, parsley, black peppercorns, and enough water to cover it by 1 inch. Bring the water to a boil, lower the heat, and simmer the chicken, skimming occasionally, for 45 to 60 minutes or until the chicken is thoroughly cooked. Remove the chicken from the broth; when it is cool enough to handle, separate the flesh from the bones and skin. (Return the bones and skin to the pot, continue simmering for one hour, and then strain the broth and reserve it for another use.) Cut the chicken meat into 1-inch pieces and set it aside in the refrigerator. Melt the 4 tablespoons of butter in a wide, deep skillet and when it is foaming, add the remaining 1 yellow onion, the remaining 3 ribs celery, the red bell pepper, green bell pepper, and apples. Sauté for 10 to 12 minutes or until they are softened. Stir in the curry powder, 1 teaspoon salt, and cayenne and cook for 1 minute. Add the apple juice to the skillet and cook until it has nearly evaporated. Remove the skillet from the heat. Melt the

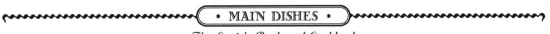
remaining 2 tablespoons of butter in a small saucepan and when it foams, whisk in the flour to make a roux, stirring constantly for 2 minutes. Do not let the roux take on any color. Slowly whisk in the half-and-half, stirring constantly to avoid lumps—this makes a béchamel. Turn the heat to low and simmer the béchamel for 5 minutes. Stir in the remaining salt.

Preheat the oven to 350°F. In a large bowl, combine the diced chicken, the sautéed vegetables and apples, the béchamel, the parsley, and the pickle relish. Stir to mix well. Transfer the mixture to a buttered, 2-quart baking dish. Spread the breadcrumbs over the top, dot with the pea-sized butter, and bake for 30 minutes or until the breadcrumb topping is browned and the hash is bubbling hot.

MAKES 6 SERVINGS

JAMAICAN JERK-RUBBED CHICKEN BREASTS
with Black Beans, Plantains and Papaya Salsa

This is a vibrantly colored dish with the bright flavors of the tropics.

6	*(8-ounce) chicken breast halves*
1½	*cups Jamaican Jerk Rub (page 114)*
3	*cups cooked Black Beans (page 117), heated*
¼	*cup Papaya Salsa (page 110)*
2	*green plantains, prepared as Fried Plantain Chips (page 123)*

Marinate the chicken in the Jamaican Jerk Rub for at least 4 hours, preferably overnight. Heat a gas or charcoal grill to medium hot. Grill the chicken skin side down for 7 to 8 minutes, until the skin is crisp and the marinade is nicely browned. Turn the breasts over and continue cooking for 6 minutes longer. Ladle 1/2 cup of hot black beans into the centers of 6 dinner plates. Place a chicken breast in the middle and spoon 1/4 cup of papaya salsa over it. Lay the plantain chips around the edges of the plate and serve.

MAKES 6 SERVINGS

Brendan Orr, Sous-Chef

Brendan Orr grew up in Miami but came to Key West only three years ago after spending time as a chef in Paris. "I learned tons over there," he says. "I was cooking French, and every once in a while I tried to throw something Caribbean at them. That didn't go over too well. I didn't go over too well myself. To be an American chef in Paris is a stigma. They said, 'What do we need an American for? What are you going to cook for us? Hamburgers?'"

Much as he learned in Paris, Brendan was eager to find a place where he was freer to play with new ideas in the kitchen. He and his wife wanted an opportunity to develop their talents, but not in a big city. After they returned from France late in 1998, Key West seemed the perfect home and Louie's an ideal place to practice their craft.

"Doug is so great to work for," Brendan says, "because he encourages all of us to bring in new ideas. This is a place where you can play with your food." When we spoke to him in the summer of 2002, Brendan was working with some fine Hawaiian pink snapper being flown in twice a week. One evening's recipe called for it to be rubbed with curry and five-spice powder, presented atop a tamarind butter sauce, accompanied by basmati rice and asparagus. Brendan explained that the Hawaiian snapper wasn't as fine-flaked as local yellowtail, but had a subtly different flavor that was inspiration for his spice rubs.

DESSERTS

Banana Rum Ice Cream

Black Currant Crème Brûlée

Chocolate Ice Cream

Caramel Walnut Sauce

Chocolate Banana Crème Caramel

Caramelized Bananas

Chocolate Brownie Crème Brûlée

Warm Dark Chocolate Strudel

Chocolate Pecan Brownies

Dark Chocolate Wafers

Cinnamon Bread Pudding

Compote of Golden Pineapple

Crystallized Blueberries

Ginger Rhubarb Cobbler

Espresso Panna Cotta

Five-Spice Biscotti

Frozen Malt Soufflé

Hazelnut Cookies

Individual Angel Food Cakes

Leatherwood Honey and Mascarpone Ice Cream

Niall's Gingersnap Key Lime Pie

Pear Frangipane Tart

Pear Sherbet

Pouring Cream

Rosewater Sorbet

Shredded Phyllo "Cakes"

Three Fruit Coulis

Vanilla Bean Ice Cream

BANANA RUM ICE CREAM

This is part of Louie's Banana Split, but it doesn't have to be. The ice cream makers available today for home use make it very easy to whip up a batch at a moment's notice.

6	*extra large egg yolks*
1	*cup milk*
1	*cup cream*
⅔	*cup sugar*
	Pinch of salt
1	*vanilla bean, split lengthwise*
2	*puréed overripe bananas*
½	*cup dark rum*

Place the egg yolks in a mixing bowl. Combine the milk, cream, sugar, salt, and vanilla bean in a saucepan and bring the mixture to a boil over medium heat. Slowly whisk the hot liquid into the egg yolks to temper them and return the mixture to the saucepan. Place the pan over medium heat and begin stirring immediately with a rubber spatula, scraping the sides and bottom of the pan continuously so the egg won't adhere and form lumps.

Cook the custard until it thickens enough to lightly coat the spatula and then pour it into a mixing bowl set in a larger bowl of ice. Allow the mixture to cool completely. Stir in the bananas and rum. Freeze the mixture in an ice cream machine according to the manufacturer's instructions.

MAKES 1 QUART

BLACK CURRANT CRÈME BRÛLÉE

Crème Brûlé is a favorite restaurant dessert everywhere, but it's not too difficult to make at home. Small butane torches are available at fine houseware stores or specialty kitchen stores, or the custards with their sugar topping can be put closely under a broiler to brown the sugar topping. We flavored this with black currant purée to give it a slight tartness and beautiful color. Raspberry Purée would work as well. Dark Chocolate Wafers served along with the custards provide a pleasant crunch.

2	plus 2 cups heavy cream
1¼	cups sugar
¾	cup black currant purée
12	extra large egg yolks
1	teaspoon vanilla extract
1	to 1½ cups sugar for topping

Preheat the oven to 325°F. Bring 2 cups of the cream to a boil in a saucepan and remove it from the heat. Whisk in the sugar to dissolve it completely. Add the purée and the remaining 2 cups cream, followed by the egg yolks and vanilla. Whisk thoroughly and strain the mixture through a fine-mesh sieve. Pour the mixture into individual custard cups or soufflé dishes. Set the cups or dishes in a pan of hot water and bake in the oven for 35 to 40 minutes or until the custard is set. Let the custards cool briefly; then chill them thoroughly in the refrigerator.

To serve, cover the top of each custard with 2 to 3 tablespoons sugar. Aim the flame of a propane or butane torch directly at the sugar until it melts, bubbles, and caramelizes. Serve immediately with Dark Chocolate Wafers (page 179).

MAKES 8 SERVINGS

Niall Bowen, Pastry Chef

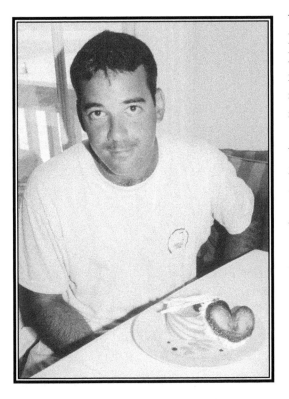

When you ask Pastry Chef Niall Bowen what brought him to Key West from his native New England, he has an immediate one-word answer: Tarpon.

He cannot really say whether he loves sport fishing or baking better. Since he was sixteen years old, he knew that what he wanted to do in life was bake. And he has always loved to fish. So here he is on Key West, baking beautiful desserts for Louie's Backyard in the morning and catching eighty-five-pound tarpon later in the day. "I love my life," he says. "I am the luckiest guy I know."

Niall says that it wasn't until 1998 that Louie's started serving Key lime pie for dessert. The recipe for Louie's pie is unique because instead of the traditional graham cracker crust, it uses a zippier gingersnap crust (see page 189). It was added to the menu by popular demand—so many visitors to the Keys demand Key lime pie.

The pie's popularity causes Niall to compete against himself. "I try to sell other desserts," he says, "But it is tough to go against Key lime pie. I do a totally untraditional dobos tort in which I use ganache instead of chocolate buttercream. I like that because it is cool on the palate. Here in the Keys, cool counts for a lot."

CHOCOLATE ICE CREAM

Beware of this one. It's dangerous.

CUSTARD:

6	*extra large egg yolks*
1	*cup milk*
1	*cup cream*
⅔	*cup sugar*
	Pinch of salt
1	*vanilla bean, split lengthwise*

CREAM:

1½	*cups milk*
4	*ounces dark chocolate, finely chopped*
⅓	*cup unsweetened cocoa powder, sifted*
¼	*cup sugar*
⅔	*cup light corn syrup*

To make the custard, place the egg yolks in a mixing bowl. Combine the milk, cream, sugar, salt, and vanilla bean in a saucepan and bring to a boil over medium heat. Slowly whisk the hot liquid into the egg yolks to temper them and then return the mixture to the saucepan. Place the pan over medium heat and begin stirring immediately with a rubber spatula, scraping the sides and bottom of the pan continuously so the egg won't adhere and form lumps. Cook the custard until it thickens enough to lightly coat the spatula and then pour it into a mixing bowl set in a larger bowl of ice. Allow the mixture to cool completely. Remove the vanilla bean.

To make the cream, bring the milk to a boil in a small saucepan. Remove the pan from the heat and whisk in the chocolate, cocoa, sugar, and corn syrup. Stir until the mixture is homogeneous. Strain the mixture through a fine-mesh sieve and combine it with the vanilla custard. Cool the mixture and freeze it in an ice cream machine according to the manufacturer's instructions.

MAKES ABOUT 2 ½ PINTS

CARAMEL WALNUT SAUCE

Chocolate Ice Cream, Banana Rum Ice Cream, Vanilla Bean Ice Cream, and this sauce go together to make one amazing banana split!

¾	cup walnut pieces
¼	cup sugar
1¼	cups water
2	tablespoons butter
¾	cup light brown sugar
1	cup heavy cream
	Pinch of salt
1½	teaspoons vanilla extract

Combine the walnuts, sugar, and water in a small saucepan and simmer for 15 minutes. Drain the walnuts, discarding the liquid, and set the nuts aside. Combine the butter and brown sugar in a heavy-bottomed saucepan with enough water just to wet the sugar. Cook over medium-high heat, stirring occasionally, until the mixture darkens slightly and gives off an aroma of caramel. Remove the pan from the heat and slowly add the cream, stirring with a long-handled whisk. This process will cause a lot of steam to rise all at once, along with some bubbling and spattering of the hot sauce. Work carefully while adding the cream, keeping your hands and face away from the rising steam. When all of the cream has been added, stir in the salt, vanilla, and the walnuts. Cool the sauce completely in the refrigerator. Thin the sauce if necessary with additional cream, adding it 1 teaspoon at a time.

MAKES ABOUT 4 CUPS

CHOCOLATE BANANA CRÈME CARAMEL

The subtle, delicate texture of the custard is offset by the big bold flavors of chocolate and banana. Five-Spice Biscotti, served alongside, provides complementary flavors and a satisfying, contrasting crunch.

CARAMEL:

1½	*cups sugar*
	Water as needed

CUSTARD:

1	*plus 1 cup milk*
½	*cup sugar*
2	*ounces finely chopped dark chocolate*

1	*large, overripe banana*
2	*ounces heavy cream*
1	*teaspoon vanilla extract*
3	*extra large eggs*
4	*extra large egg yolks*

Preheat the oven to 300°F.

To make the caramel, place the sugar in a heavy-bottomed pan and add enough water to the pan to cover the sugar. Cook over high heat until the sugar is a medium brown. Immediately pour the caramel into six 1-cup ramekins or custard cups, coating the bottom of each dish with a quarter-inch layer of caramel. Set the custard cups aside. (To clean the pan, allow the remaining caramel to cool, add several inches of water to the pan, and bring the water to a boil, covered. The caramel will dissolve in the water.)

To make the custard, bring 1 cup of the milk to a boil in a saucepan. Remove the pan from the heat and mix in the sugar and chocolate, stirring until the sugar has dissolved and the chocolate has melted. Purée the banana in a food processor and add it with the remaining 1 cup milk, the cream, and vanilla to the saucepan. Whisk in the eggs and egg yolks and strain the mixture through a medium-mesh sieve. Divide the mixture between the caramel-lined custard cups, filling them to within half an inch of the top.

Place the cups in a baking pan and add water to the pan to reach halfway up the sides of the cups. Bake in the oven for 45 to 60 minutes or until the custard is set. The custard should not rise or puff at all. Remove the custards from the oven, allow them to cool slightly, and refrigerate them until thoroughly chilled.

To serve, slide the blade of a paring knife between the sides of the cup and the custard. Place a dessert plate upside down over the custard cup. Invert the plate and the cup together and give them a firm shake or two. The custard should slip from its baking dish with its caramel coating on top. Pour any remaining caramel from the dish onto the plate. Serve with Five-Spice Biscotti (page 184).

MAKES 6 SERVINGS

CARAMELIZED BANANAS

These are also a delicious addition to a bowl of ice cream, and would make a nice embellishment for the Chocolate Banana Crème Caramel (page 174).

---

8   *small bananas (Cuban finger bananas if possible)*

1   *cup sugar*

Peel the bananas, split them lengthwise, and place them cut side up on a flame-proof baking sheet. Cover each banana half with a generous layer of sugar. Point the flame of a propane or butane torch directly at the sugar until it liquefies, bubbles, and browns. Serve immediately with the Frozen Malt Soufflés (page 185).

MAKES 8 SERVINGS

CHOCOLATE BROWNIE CRÈME BRÛLÉE

This is the invention of Louie's original pastry chef, Susan Porter, and it remains one of the best-selling desserts we've ever offered. The rich custard can be baked and served as a classic vanilla crème brûlé, but the surprise of finding that incredible chocolate brownie hidden at the bottom of the dish makes this a truly memorable dessert.

3¼	*cups heavy cream*
1	*vanilla bean, split in half*
9	*extra large egg yolks*
½	*cup sugar plus 1 cup for the topping*
8	*(2-inch-square) Chocolate Pecan Brownies (page 178)*

Preheat the oven to 325°F. Combine the cream and vanilla bean in a saucepan and bring to a simmer over medium-high heat. Beat the egg yolks lightly with the ½ cup sugar in a mixing bowl. Slowly pour the scalded cream into the egg yolk mixture, whisking constantly, and then pour the custard back into the saucepan and return it to the heat. Cook the custard, stirring constantly, until it thickens enough to coat the back of a wooden spoon. Don't let the custard boil. Immediately strain the custard through a medium-mesh sieve into a bowl. Push the Chocolate Pecan Brownies into the bottoms of eight 6-ounce custard cups. Fill the cups to within ½ inch of the top with the custard. Place the cups in a pan and add hot water to reach halfway up the sides of the cups. Bake in the oven for 30 to 40 minutes or until the custard is just set. Remove the custards from the oven and chill them thoroughly in the refrigerator.

To serve, sprinkle 1 to 2 tablespoons of granulated sugar over the surface of each custard in an even layer. Aim the flame of a propane or butane torch directly at the sugar until it melts, bubbles, and caramelizes. Serve at once.

MAKES 8 SERVINGS

WARM DARK CHOCOLATE STRUDEL

We serve this with a Compote of Golden Pineapple and Kaffir Lime Leaves. The juxtaposition of flavors is remarkable, but the strudels are delicious served just by themselves.

FILLING:

¾	*cup milk*
6	*ounces dark chocolate, finely chopped*
1	*teaspoon vanilla extract*
3	*cups chocolate cake crumbs*
2	*ounces dark chocolate, roughly chopped*

STRUDEL:

½	*package frozen phyllo sheets, thoroughly thawed*
2	*cups clarified butter, melted (or more as needed)*

Preheat the oven to 375°F. Bring the milk to a boil and remove it from the heat. Whisk in the finely chopped chocolate until smooth. Stir in the vanilla extract and let the mixture cool for 10 minutes. Place the cake crumbs in a bowl and pour the chocolate mixture over them. Stir gently with a wooden spoon until the crumbs and chocolate are evenly combined. Stir in the roughly chopped chocolate and chill the mixture until it is firm enough to be shaped by hand. Form the filling into six balls and refrigerate them for at least 30 minutes. Lay the sheets of phyllo on a cutting board and cut them with a sharp knife into six stacks of 2 x 9-inch strips. Cover the strips with a clean, dry towel to keep them from drying out as you work. Lay one strip of phyllo on the cutting board and brush it liberally with the clarified butter. Lay a second strip overlapping the first diagonally, crossing in the center and with the ends of each strip just touching. Brush the second strip with the butter. Continue adding overlapping strips, buttering each one, until the stacked strips form a complete circle. Place a ball of chocolate filling in the center of the circle. Starting with the last strip of phyllo put in place, lift the ends of the strip and bring them up over the filling, twisting them gently together at the top. Repeat with the remaining strips, in order, until the filling is completely enclosed and the ends of the phyllo strips form a flower-like design at the top. Place the strudel on a parchment-lined baking sheet and brush it gently with clarified butter. Repeat with the remaining phyllo and chocolate filling. Bake the strudels in the preheated oven for 10 to 12 minutes or until they are nicely browned and the filling is hot. Serve warm with the Compote of Golden Pineapple (page 181).

MAKES 6 SERVINGS

CHOCOLATE PECAN BROWNIES

This is a terrific brownie recipe. The pecans can be replaced with walnuts or the brownies can be made with no nuts at all.

9	*ounces dark chocolate, finely chopped*
6	*ounces unsalted butter, cut into ½-inch pieces*
1¼	*cups sugar*
1	*teaspoon vanilla*
1	*teaspoon salt*
3	*extra large eggs*
¼	*cup all-purpose flour*
1¾	*cups chopped pecans*

Preheat the oven to 350°F. Melt the chocolate and butter in a mixing bowl set over a pan of simmering water, stirring to combine them well. Whisk in the sugar, followed by the vanilla, salt, eggs (one at a time), and the flour. Stir in the pecans. Spread the mixture evenly in a buttered and floured 9 x 13-inch baking pan. Bake in the oven for 25 to 30 minutes or until the edges of the cake pull away slightly from the sides of the pan and the center is just firm. Do not overbake. Remove the pan from the oven and allow it to cool before cutting the brownies into squares.

MAKES 16 TO 20 SQUARES

DARK CHOCOLATE WAFERS

These cookies are delicious, and not too sweet. We cut them into circles of various sizes to place on the plates around the Black Currant Crème Brûlé.

6	*tablespoons butter at room temperature*
½	*cup sugar*
2	*ounces dark chocolate, melted*
	Pinch of salt
1½	*cups flour*
½	*cup unsweetened cocoa powder, sifted*
1	*extra large egg*
1	*teaspoon vanilla*

Preheat the oven to 350°F. In a large bowl cream the butter, sugar, melted chocolate, and salt until there are no lumps at all. Add the flour, cocoa, egg, and vanilla and mix to form a smooth dough. (If the dough is too soft to roll out, refrigerate it briefly to firm it.) Roll the dough on a lightly floured surface to a thickness of ⅛ inch. Use a small round cutter to cut the dough into circles and place the circles on a parchment-lined baking sheet. Bake in the oven until crisp, about 15 minutes.

MAKES 5 DOZEN 2-INCH CIRCLES

CINNAMON BREAD PUDDING
with Roasted Pecans and Brandied Cherries

Using croissants rather than white bread for this pudding adds a richness and a texture that's hard to beat. We bake this in extra large muffin tins for individual servings, but it works just as well baked as a loaf and sliced. Serve it warm with Pouring Cream.

1	plus 1¼ cups heavy cream	2	teaspoons vanilla extract
1	tablespoon ground cinnamon	1½	cups fancy pecan halves
¾	cup sugar	4	large croissants
¾	cup egg yolks	¾	cup brandied cherries
¼	cup egg whites		
	Pinch of salt		

Preheat the oven to 350°F. Bring 1 cup of the cream to a boil with the cinnamon, remove it from the heat, and whisk in the sugar until it has dissolved. Add the remaining cream, then the egg yolks and whites, whisking them in thoroughly. Add the salt and vanilla. Strain the custard through a medium-mesh sieve. Spread the pecan halves on a baking sheet and toast them in the oven for 10 minutes or until they are slightly darkened and fragrant. Cut the croissants into 1½-inch pieces and place them in a large bowl with the pecans and cherries. Pour the warm custard over the croissant mixture and press down lightly to encourage the bread to absorb the custard. Let the mixture stand for 10 minutes. Line a 6-cup loaf pan with plastic wrap, pushing the wrap down into the corners of the pan and using enough to allow at least 4 inches of overhang. Fill the pan with the pudding mixture, sprinkle the top lightly with granulated sugar, and place the pan in a larger pan. Add hot water to reach two-thirds of the way up the sides of the pudding pan and place the whole business in the oven. Bake the pudding for 30 to 40 minutes, until it is puffed, browned, and firm to the touch. Remove the pudding and its water bath from the oven and allow it to cool slightly. Unmold the pudding by pulling on an edge of the plastic and removing the wrap completely. Slice the pudding and serve it warm with Pouring Cream (page 193).

MAKES 8 SERVINGS

COMPOTE OF GOLDEN PINEAPPLE
with Kaffir Lime Leaves

The leaves of the Kaffir lime tree are extraordinarily fragrant and very hard to come by. An acceptable substitute would be the zest of a lime cut into fine shreds and blanched in boiling water for 30 seconds.

½	*large, ripe golden pineapple*
4	*or 5 fresh Kaffir lime leaves*
1	*cup sugar*
	Pinch of salt

Peel the pineapple, remove the core, and cut the flesh into ½-inch cubes. Place the pineapple in a bowl. Remove the tough central vein from the lime leaves and cut each leaf into very fine slivers. Stir the lime leaves, sugar, and salt into the pineapple and chill the mixture for 24 hours before serving.

MAKES 3 CUPS

CRYSTALLIZED BLUEBERRIES

These are easy to make and addictive to eat.

1	*pint fresh blueberries*
½	*cup egg whites*
2	*cups sugar*

Pick over the blueberries to eliminate any stems or bruised berries. Beat the egg whites with a wire whisk just enough to break them up. Place the sugar in a separate bowl. Toss the blueberries with the egg whites to coat them completely and then drain them in a wire strainer. The berries should be lightly coated, shiny and wet looking. While the berries are still wet, toss them five or six at a time in the sugar. Place the sugared berries, not touching, on a parchment-lined sheet pan. Let the berries dry overnight in a cool, dry room.

MAKES 2 CUPS

GINGER RHUBARB COBBLER

Served hot with a scoop of homemade ice cream, this traditional American dessert is a favorite of ours.

STREUSEL TOPPING:

½	cup unsalted butter
½	cup dark brown sugar
½	cup all-purpose flour
¼	cup oats
¼	cup sliced almonds
1	teaspoon vanilla extract
	Pinch of salt

RHUBARB FILLING:

¼	cup salted butter
1¼	pounds fresh rhubarb, cut into 1-inch pieces
1	tablespoon grated fresh ginger
1	vanilla bean, split lengthwise
1½	cups sugar
1	large or 2 small oranges

Preheat the oven to 365°F. To make the streusel, cut the butter into ½-inch pieces and place it in a mixing bowl. Check the brown sugar to be sure there are no stiff lumps and add it to the bowl with the flour, oats, almonds, vanilla, and salt. Work the mixture together with a wooden spoon until the butter is evenly distributed but the texture is still crumbly. Be careful not to overmix it. Store the streusel in the refrigerator or freezer until needed.

To make the filling, melt the butter in a large sauté pan over medium heat; then stir in the rhubarb and ginger. Cook, stirring often, for 10 minutes or until the rhubarb has begun to soften. Be careful not to let the butter or ginger brown. Add the vanilla bean and sugar to the pan and, working directly over the pan, remove the zest from the oranges with a zester. (The orange oil released by zesting adds flavor to the filling). Stir well. Squeeze the oranges and add the juice to the pan. Cook the mixture until the rhubarb is soft, but not falling apart. Immediately strain the mixture, removing the vanilla bean. Set the rhubarb aside and return the liquid to the pan. Continue to

simmer the liquid for about 10 minutes or until it has reduced by half; then pour it back over the cooked rhubarb. Place the filling in individual 1-cup ramekins or in a 2-quart casserole. Cover the top of the cobbler generously with the streusel and place it in the preheated oven. Bake about 20 minutes, until the topping is well browned and the filling is piping hot, but do not allow the filling to boil.

Serve hot with vanilla ice cream.

MAKES 6 TO 8 SERVINGS

ESPRESSO PANNA COTTA

A two-part Italian or Spanish stovetop espresso maker is perfect for brewing the coffee needed to flavor this dessert. Instant espresso, dissolved in water according to the package directions, can be substituted, but the flavor and aroma won't be so rich.

¾	*cup freshly brewed espresso*
3	*cups heavy cream*
1	*cup milk*
1½	*cups confectioners' sugar*
2	*teaspoons powdered gelatin*

Combine the espresso, cream, milk, and sugar in a saucepan over high heat and bring the mixture to a boil. Lower the heat so the mixture just simmers and cook for 8 to 10 minutes, stirring occasionally. Remove the pan from the heat. Dissolve the gelatin into the hot milk. Pour the mixture into six plastic-wrap-lined custard cups, let it cool, and refrigerate until set, about 4 hours. When the panna cotta have set, invert each cup onto a Hazelnut Cookie (page 186) set on a dessert plate. Lift away the cup, peel off the plastic wrap, and serve the panna cotta drizzled with orange sauce.

MAKES 6 SERVINGS

FIVE-SPICE BISCOTTI

Anise is the traditional seasoning for these twice-baked cookies. The predominant flavor of these Chinese Five Spice Powder is star anise; but its undertones of cinnamon, clove, and Szechuan pepercorn make for a more exotic flavor.

¼	cup butter at room temperature
1¾	cups bread flour
1	teaspoon baking powder
2	teaspoons Chinese five-spice powder
2	extra large eggs
	Pinch of salt
⅔	cup granulated sugar
1	teaspoon vanilla extract

Preheat the oven to 325°F. Place the butter, flour, baking powder, and five-spice powder in a large bowl. Rub the butter into the dry ingredients with a wooden spoon until there are no lumps at all. The mixture should be dry and crumbly; if overmixed it will form a paste that will not allow the eggs to be properly mixed in. In a separate bowl, whisk the eggs with the salt, sugar, and vanilla to dissolve the sugar and aerate the eggs. Pour the egg mixture over the butter and flour mixture and stir with a wooden spoon until the dough comes together. Form the dough into a log about 2 inches wide and 1 inch high on a parchment-lined baking sheet and place it in the oven for 25 to 30 minutes or until it is lightly browned on the surface and firm in the center. Remove the log from the oven and allow it to cool. Increase the temperature of the oven to 350°F. When the log is cool enough to handle, cut it into ⅓-inch slices and place them standing on edge on the baking sheet. Return the cookies to the oven and bake them for 12 to 15 minutes longer or until they are dry and nicely browned around the edges. Cool the biscotti completely before serving.

MAKES 16 TO 20 BISCOTTI

FROZEN MALT SOUFFLÉ

At the restaurant, we use sections of PVC pipe—three inches high with a three-inch diameter—for molding these and other cold desserts.

1	cup malt powder
	Pinch of salt
	Water as needed
⅓	cup sugar
1	tablespoon vanilla extract
6	extra large egg yolks
1¼	cups heavy cream
1¼	cups toasted macadamia nuts

Combine the malt powder and salt in a small saucepan and add enough water to the pan to just cover the malt. Whisk the ingredients together and cook over medium heat, stirring often until the mixture comes to a boil. When the mixture boils, cook until the mixture becomes thin and translucent, stirring constantly to avoid scorching, about 2 minutes. Remove the pan from the heat and whisk in the sugar and vanilla. Transfer the mixture to a bowl and allow it to cool completely. When the malt syrup is cool, place the egg yolks in a separate bowl and beat them with a wire whisk until they are airy and lemon colored and form a "ribbon" on top of themselves when dropped from the whisk. In a separate bowl beat the cream until it forms soft peaks. Gently whisk the cool malt syrup into the cream and then fold in the egg yolks. Line eight cups of a large muffin tin, or eight individual soufflé dishes with plastic wrap, fitting it down carefully into the corners of the molds. Place six or seven macadamia nuts in each mold and carefully fill the molds with the soufflé mixture, leveling off the tops. Freeze the soufflés for at least 4 hours before unmolding and serving, nut side up, with Caramelized Bananas (page 175).

MAKES 8 INDIVIDUAL SOUFFLÉS

HAZELNUT COOKIES

The flavor of these cookies is a perfect foil for the rich coffee taste of the Espresso Panna Cotta (page 183).

1	*cup ground hazelnuts*
¼	*cup butter at room temperature*
1	*extra large egg*
1	*cup confectioners' sugar, sifted*
	Grated zest of 1 orange
	Pinch of salt
1	*teaspoon vanilla extract*

Preheat the oven to 350°F. Combine the hazelnuts, butter, egg, sugar, zest, salt, and vanilla until well blended. Form the dough into mounds of 2 tablespoons each on parchment-lined baking sheets and bake for 8 to 10 minutes or until the cookies are flattened and evenly browned. Allow the cookies to cool before removing them from the pans.

MAKES ABOUT 18 COOKIES

INDIVIDUAL ANGEL FOOD CAKES

This recipe can also be baked in a traditional angel food cake pan, but an individual cake is more "special," and makes a great perch for the scoop of sorbet. We serve this with three different fruit coulis (page 195)—Raspberry, Apricot, and Blueberry—that are "painted" on the plate with plastic squeeze bottles, along with fresh berries. Edible flowers, particularly pansies or roses, make a terrific garnish.

5	*extra large egg whites*
¾	*cup sugar*
	Pinch of salt
½	*teaspoon vanilla extract*
½	*cup cake flour*
	Confectioners' sugar for dusting

Preheat the oven to 365°F. Place the egg whites, sugar, salt, and vanilla in a mixing bowl set over a pan of simmering water and stir them until the mixture is just a bit warmer than body temperature. Remove from the heat and beat the mixture with a wire whisk or an electric mixer until soft peaks form. Sift the cake flour and fold it very gently into the egg whites, mixing just until the flour is incorporated. Pour the mixture into eight clean, ungreased muffin cups, filling them three-fourths full. Bake the cakes in the oven for 10 to 12 minutes or until they are browned on the top and the centers spring back when pressed with a finger. Remove the pans from the oven and invert them on a rack until cool. Carefully unmold the cakes, cutting between the sides of the pans and the cakes with a paring knife to release them. Dust the cakes with powdered sugar and carefully cut a small circle from the top of each. Serve the cakes topped with a scoop of Rosewater Sorbet (page 193) and surrounded by fresh mixed berries.

MAKES 8 SERVINGS

LEATHERWOOD HONEY AND MASCARPONE ICE CREAM

This ice cream is made with mascarpone, an ultra-rich Italian cream cheese, and Leatherwood Honey, which has a bright, floral taste and lends a unique, haunting flavor to the dessert. We serve it on a "cake" of shredded phyllo with crystallized blueberries and blueberry coulis.

1	pound mascarpone
¾	cup milk
1¼	cup water
¾	cup Tasmanian Leatherwood Honey
½	cup light corn syrup
2	teaspoons vanilla extract
	Pinch of salt

Place the mascarpone in a mixing bowl. In a separate bowl, mix the milk, water, honey, corn syrup, vanilla, and salt together with a wire whisk. Gradually beat the mixture into the mascarpone, a little at a time, whisking well after each addition to form a smooth mixture with no lumps. Strain the ice cream base through a medium-mesh sieve and freeze it in an ice cream maker according to the manufacturer's directions.

MAKES ABOUT 1½ QUARTS

NIALL'S GINGERSNAP KEY LIME PIE

Our not-so-traditional gingersnap crust makes a nice balance between the sweet/tart filling and the spice and crunch of the crust. We serve it with fresh raspberries and raspberry coulis.

CRUST:

⅔	cup sugar
1	cup butter at room temperature
	Pinch of salt
3¼	cups all-purpose flour
2	extra large eggs
1	teaspoon vanilla
¼	cup molasses
1	tablespoon ground ginger
½	teaspoon ground cinnamon

FILLING:

1	(14-ounce) can sweetened condensed milk
½	cup key lime juice
4	extra large egg yolks
1	teaspoon vanilla extract

Preheat the oven to 325°F. To make the crust, cream the sugar, butter, and salt in a large bowl until smooth and homogenous. Add the flour, eggs, vanilla, molasses, ginger, and cinnamon and mix to form a smooth dough. Roll the dough on a lightly floured surface into a circle about 13 inches across and ¼ inch thick. Line a 9-inch pie tin or a tart pan with a removable bottom with the dough and trim the excess. Bake the crust for 12 to 15 minutes or until nicely browned. Thoroughly combine the condensed milk, lime juice, egg yolks, and vanilla for the filling, stirring with a wire whisk. Pour the filling into the pie shell and place the pie in the oven until the filling has set like a soft custard, about 15 minutes. Cool the pie completely before cutting and serving with Raspberry Coulis (page 195).

MAKES 8 SERVINGS

PEAR FRANGIPANE TART

This is a traditional French tart, very good on its own, even better with cool Pear Sherbet and Apricot Coulis.

CRUST:

1	cup unsalted butter at room temperature
⅔	cup sugar
	Pinch of salt
3¼	cups all-purpose flour
2	extra large eggs
1	teaspoon vanilla extract

FRANGIPANE:

½	cup unsalted butter
1¼	cups ground, natural almonds (not blanched)
½	cup sugar
	Grated zest of one orange (2 teaspoons)
	Pinch of salt
1½	teaspoon vanilla extract
1	teaspoon almond extract
4	extra large eggs

PEARS:

4	firm but ripe pears
1	cup white wine
1½	cups water
¼	cup honey
½	cup sugar
1	whole vanilla bean
4	whole cloves
½	of a whole nutmeg
½	cup strained apricot preserves, melted
¼	cup toasted sliced almonds

To make the crust, cream the butter, sugar, and salt until the ingredients are homogeneous. Be careful not to overmix. Add the flour, eggs, and vanilla all together and stir the mixture to form a firm dough. If the dough is too soft, refrigerate it briefly to firm it before rolling it out. Roll the dough into a circle ¼ inch thick on a lightly floured board. Fit the dough into a 9-inch tart pan with a removable bottom, trim the edges to fit, and set the tart shell in the refrigerator.

To make the frangipane, beat the butter, ground almonds, sugar, orange zest, and salt

in a bowl until no lumps of butter remain. Add the vanilla and almond extracts and the eggs, one at a time, mixing each addition thoroughly before adding the next.

To poach the pears, peel them, cut them in half, and remove the cores. Place the pear halves in a saucepan with the wine, water, honey, sugar, vanilla bean, cloves, and nutmeg. Cover the pan, place it over medium heat, and slowly bring the liquid to a bare simmer. Cook the pears until they are soft throughout without allowing the liquid to approach the boiling point, but not so tender that they fall apart, about 25 to 30 minutes. Remove the pears from their poaching liquid with a slotted spoon and set them aside to cool.

Preheat the oven to 325°F. To assemble the tart, spread the frangipane in an even layer, about ⅔-inch thick, in the prepared tart shell. Cut each pear half into thin slices and place them on top of the frangipane, arranging them in a circle of fanned-out slices. Bake the tart for 25 to 30 minutes or until the pears and the edges of the crust are nicely browned and the frangipane has begun to puff around the edges of the tart. Brush the warm tart with the melted apricot glaze and sprinkle the sliced almonds evenly over the top. Serve warm or at room temperature with Pear Sherbet (page 192) and Apricot Coulis (page 195).

MAKES 8 SERVINGS

PEAR SHERBET

We serve this with the Pear Tart, but it's good enough to make for its own sake. Try it drizzled with Dark Chocolate Sauce.

1	*cup water*
1	*cup sugar*
2	*pears, poached as for the Pear Frangipane Tart (page 190), puréed and strained (about 1 cup purée)*
1	*cup milk*
	Pinch of salt
1½	*tablespoons lemon juice*
1	*teaspoon vanilla extract*
½	*cup light corn syrup*

Bring the water to a boil and remove it from the heat. Whisk in the sugar until it has completely dissolved. Stir in the pears, milk, salt, lemon juice, vanilla, and corn syrup. Cool the mixture completely and freeze it in an ice cream machine according to the manufacturer's directions.

MAKES ABOUT 1 QUART

POURING CREAM

This is just heavy cream whipped enough to thicken it slightly. It's perfect poured over a serving of warm cobbler, where it slowly melts into the fruit.

1	cup heavy cream
1	tablespoon sugar
½	teaspoon vanilla extract

Combine the cream, sugar, and vanilla in a medium mixing bowl and beat with a wire whisk until it just begins to thicken. The cream should hold its shape slightly but still be soft enough to pour. Serve right away.

MAKES 1½ CUPS

ROSEWATER SORBET

The rosewater flavor is very strong. Don't be tempted to use more than the recipe indicates. A tiny drop of red or pink food coloring can be added to give the sorbet a rose-colored blush.

1½	cups water
1	cup light corn syrup
½	teaspoon rose water
⅛	teaspoon vanilla extract

Stir the water, corn syrup, rose water, and vanilla together and freeze them in an ice cream maker according to the manufacturer's directions.

MAKES 1½ PINTS

SHREDDED PHYLLO "CAKES"

Shredded phyllo, also called Kataifi, is available in specialty food shops and some grocery stores. It's cut by machine into extremely fine threads that approach the texture of shredded wheat when baked. These "cakes" can also be used as the base for an unusual fruit shortcake.

12	ounces Kataifi (shredded phyllo dough)
1¼	cups warm clarified butter
¾	cup Tasmanian Leatherwood Honey

Preheat the oven to 350°F. Divide the kataifi into six equal portions and cover them with a clean, dry kitchen towel. Combine the butter and honey in a mixing bowl, whisking vigorously; then immediately add one portion of the kataifi and turn it over in the mixture to coat it well before the two liquids naturally separate. Lift the coated kataifi out of the butter-honey mixture and allow the excess to drain back into the bowl. Place the kataifi on a parchment-lined baking sheet and shape it into a round disc about ½ inch thick. Repeat with the remaining portions of kataifi, whisking the butter and honey well each time. Bake the "cakes" in the oven for 12 to 15 minutes or until they are browned and crisp throughout and then cool them completely on a rack.

MAKES 6 INDIVIDUAL CAKES

THREE FRUIT COULIS

Most of the desserts at Louie's Backyard are served with one, two, or even all three of these simple fruit sauces.

APRICOT COULIS

½   *pound pitted fresh apricots*

1   *cup sugar*

¼   *cup water*

      Pinch of salt

In a blender or food processor, purée the apricots, sugar, water, and salt and strain through a fine-mesh sieve. Store in the refrigerator.

RASPBERRY COULIS

½   *pound fresh or frozen raspberries*

1   *cup sugar*

¼   *cup water*

⅛   *teaspoon vanilla extract*

In a blender or food processor, purée the raspberries, sugar, water, and vanilla and strain through a fine-mesh sieve. Store in the refrigerator.

BLUEBERRY COULIS

½   *pound fresh blueberries*

1   *cup sugar*

¼   *cup water*

In a blender or food processor, purée the blueberries, sugar, and water and strain through a fine-mesh sieve. Store in the refrigerator.

MAKES ABOUT 2 CUPS

VANILLA BEAN ICE CREAM

This is a very rich ice cream, which has flecks of real vanilla.

6	*extra large egg yolks*
1	*cup milk*
1	*cup cream*
⅔	*cup sugar*
1	*vanilla bean, split lengthwise*
	Pinch of salt

Place the egg yolks in a mixing bowl. Combine the milk, cream, sugar, vanilla bean, and salt in a saucepan and bring the mixture to a boil over medium heat. Slowly whisk the hot liquid into the egg yolks to temper them and then return the mixture to the saucepan. Place the pan over medium heat and begin stirring immediately with a rubber spatula, scraping the sides and bottom of the pan continuously so the egg won't adhere and form lumps.

Cook the custard until it thickens enough to lightly coat the spatula; then pour it into a mixing bowl set in a larger bowl of ice. Allow the mixture to cool completely. Freeze the mixture in an ice cream machine according to the manufacturer's directions.

MAKES 1½ PINTS

DRINKS

Chocolate Espresso Martini

Mojito

Rumrunner

Island Cosmopolitan

Pineapple Vodka

Sangria

CHOCOLATE ESPRESSO MARTINI

This is one of the best concoctions to come out of the recent martini craze. It's rich enough to call it a dessert.

1	*ounce Absolut Vodka*
1	*ounce Kahlua*
1	*ounce brewed espresso*
	Ice
	Finely grated chocolate for rimming the glass

In a blender or shaker, mix the Absolut, Kahlua, and espresso. Shake with ice until well chilled and strain into a martini glass rimmed with grated chocolate.

MAKES 1 SERVING

MOJITO

You could call this a Cuban mint julep, but it's lighter and more refreshing. It's an addictive cocktail—appealing to look at and easy to drink.

1	*tablespoon sugar*
3	*tablespoons fresh lime juice*
3	*sprigs fresh mint plus additional for garnish*
	Ice
1½	*ounces white rum*
1	*splash soda water*
2	*dashes bitters (optional)*

Put the sugar, lime juice, and mint in a tall glass and mash the mint with a wooden muddler. Add the ice, rum, the splash of soda, and bitters, if using. Garnish with additional mint.

MAKES 1 SERVING

Chris Robinson, Bartender

To be a bartender almost anywhere on Key West is an exalted position. The bartender at Louie's Backyard is an island star. His name is Chris Robinson and he has been here since the beginning. In 1972 he lived next door, downstairs at 704 Waddell; his pal Jimmy Buffett lived above him. At the time, he was tending bar at Key West's Chart Room, a place that was a kind of nerve center for the town. "Everything happened there," he recalls. "All the politicians and important people hung out at the Chart Room, and I got to know most of them."

Chris observes that thirty years ago margaritas were no big deal on the island. Rum was the favored drink—on the rocks or with tonic water. Then after 1977, when Jimmy Buffett wrote and sang "Margaritaville," sales of the symbolic drink went up tenfold. Now Chris sees that Mojitas are the big trend in libations. They were Ernest Hemingway's choice of

drink in Cuba, but they are no fun for a bartender to make. "The fresh mint goes everywhere," Chris says. "But people like them because they are so refreshing, and so strong."

Chris' late dog, Ten Speed, and Jimmy Buffett's cat, Radar, used to drink kahlúa and cream together at Louie's bar. "Ten Speed would work the deck," Chris recalls. "He was looking for food. We put a few dollars under his flea collar; he would hop up on a barstool and put both paws on the bar. But he would not drink his Kahlua and cream until the bartender put a napkin under the glass." Later in the decade, Chris and Jimmy Buffet both came to live at Louie's, at a time when it was closed, between 1979 and 1983: inexpensive lodging. When they were here, Louie's was a favorite windsurfer deck.

Chris tells us that he was married on the Afterdeck at Louie's, as were proprietors Phil and Pat Tenney. It's a favorite place for romance. "So many people propose here," he reveals. "The other day we had a guy pop the question and he must have brought one hundred roses. I remember another one who put his ring at the bottom of his girlfriend's champagne glass. She kept talking and making goo-goo eyes at him, and he kept saying, 'C'mon, drink your drink!' Finally she lifted the glass and saw the ring and accepted his proposal.

"What a great place to work!" he exults, sweeping his hands over the lamp-lit tables of the Afterdeck. "You are outside, and you are on the water. Life gets no better than this."

RUMRUNNER

Sitting in a teak chair, looking out over the Atlantic, a breeze in your hair, a Rumrunner in your hand—you could only be on the Afterdeck at Louie's Backyard. Or you could make these at home and close your eyes.

1½	ounces white rum	1	teaspoon fresh lemon juice
½	ounce blackberry brandy	1	teaspoon sugar
½	ounce banana liqueur	1	cup ice cubes
1	splash orange juice	½	ounce Bacardi 151
1	splash grenadine		

Combine the white rum, brandy, banana liqueur, orange juice, grenadine, lemon juice, sugar, and ice in the jar of a blender and blend until smooth. Pour into a hurricane glass and float the 151 on top.

MAKES 1 SERVING

ISLAND COSMOPOLITAN

Pat Tenney is responsible for putting most of the exotic drinks on the menu at Louie's, and this is one of her favorites. The pineapple flavored vodka makes this cocktail unique.

1½	ounces Pineapple Vodka (page 203)
2	tablespoons fresh lime juice
1	splash cranberry juice
	Few drops of Triple Sec

Mix the vodka, lime juice, cranberry juice, and Triple Sec in a blender or shaker. Shake with ice until well chilled. Strain into a martini glass to serve.

MAKES 1 SERVING

PINEAPPLE VODKA

| 1 | fresh pineapple, peeled and cut into 1 inch pieces |
| 1 | liter Sky vodka, or other premium brand |

Combine the pineapple and vodka in a glass container, cover and refrigerate for three days. Strain the vodka, discarding the pineapple and store the vodka in the refrigerator.

MAKES 1 LITER

SANGRIA

Sangria is a staple in Key West's Cuban restaurants. Louie's version is particularly popular in the afternoon out on the decks, when both lunchtime and the view can go on and on.

2	bottles red wine, Rioja or Chianti	1	cinnamon stick, about 3 inches long
2	Granny Smith apples, peeled, cored, and diced	¼	cup brandy
		¼	cup Grand Marnier
1	orange, peeled and diced	1	ounce sweet vermouth
1	lemon, peeled and sliced in thin rounds	⅓	cup gin
¾	cup sugar		

Mix together in a large pitcher the wine, apples, orange, lemon, sugar, cinnamon, brandy, Grand Marnier, vermouth, and gin and chill for 24 hours before serving.

Serve over ice in a wine glass, garnished with some of the fruit.

MAKES 16 TO 18 (4-OUNCE) SERVINGS

GLOSSARY

Aïoli (i-yō-lee) – This is a thick, strongly flavored garlic mayonnaise from French Provence.

Andouille (anh-doo-yuh) – A French sausage made from pork chitterlings and tripe, sliced and served cold as an hors d'oeuvre.

Bagna Cauda (BAH-nyah KOW-dah) – A sauce made of olive oil, butter, garlic and anchovies. From the Italian for "hot bath."

Béchamel (bay-sha-mel) – In French cuisine, this is a basic white sauce of milk stirred into a roux and thickened.

Carpaccio (kar-PAH-chō) – Very thin slices of raw beef fillet. It was created by Arrigo Cipriani, of Harry's Bar in Venice, in 1961.

Cavatelli (ka-vah-tel-ee) – This is pasta shaped like a tiny canoe.

Chèvre (SHEV-ruh) – French for goat, this is a goat's milk cheese that is soft and fresh, uncooked and unpressed. There are quite a few American producers of goat's cheese, although French products are more readily available. Chèvre can be shaped in logs or pyramids and sometimes is rolled in herbs, pepper or ash. Montrachet and Bucheron are well-known French Chèvres.

Chiffonade (shee-fohn-nad) – In French cuisine this is lettuce or other leaf vegetables sliced into thin strips and sautéed in butter.

Clarified butter – Butter that has been heated to separate the impurities, thus allowing their easy removal; butter so treated has a higher burning point and clearer color but less flavor. Also called *drawn butter*.

Conch (konk) – A gastropod mollusk usually eaten in chowder or salad or breaded and fried.

Fatback – Often confused with salt pork, fatback is the fresh layer of fat that runs along the animal's back. A good ole Southern delicacy.

Frangipane (franh-jhee-pan) – In French cooking this is a type of choux pastry. *Frangipane* cream, which is what Louie's Back Yard uses, is a crème pâtissière—a pastry cream made of egg yolks, flour, butter, and milk. It is used to fill cream puffs, line tarts underneath fruit, and garnish various pastries.

Gratin (gra-tinh) – Is a French word that refers to being topped with a crust of breadcrumbs, and sometimes grated cheese, and browned under a broiler.

Katsu sauce – This is a common Japanese condiment, sometimes called Japanese ketchup, that's mainly used as a sauce for foods coated in Panko-Japanese breadcrumbs and fried. It is available in Asian markets under a variety of brand names.

Lemon Grass - A type of grass with a small white bulb used in Southeast Asia where lemons do not grow. It has a subtle but distinct flavor, like bay leaf, and is used in curries, soups, and other dishes.

Manchego (mahn-CHAY-gō) - This cheese is made from sheep's milk and comes from Spain. It is molded, pressed, salted in brine, and cured. *Manchego* means in the style of La Mancha. You can use Pecorino Romano or Gruyere as a substitute.

Mandolin (manh-dō-leen) - A compact, hand-operated machine with various adjustable blades for thin to thick slicing and for julienne and French-fry cutting.

Mirin (meer-in) - A low-alcohol, sweet, golden wine made from glutinous rice. Available in all Japanese markets. Also referred to as *rice wine*.

Panna Cotta (PAHN-nah kah-tah) - This means *cooked cream* in Italian. It's a classic Italian dessert with many flavor variations.

Pecorino Romano (pek-or-EE-nō rō-MAH-nō) - This is a brand of *pecorino* (from *pecora*, meaning ewe) cheese made from sheep's milk. Other *pecorino* cheeses include *Sardo*, *Sicilaino*, or *Toxcano*.

Pernod (payr-nō) - It is a brand of anise (licorice)-flavored liqueur.

Prosciutto (prō-SHOO-tō) - Fresh Italian ham cured by salting and air-drying. The name implies that it is *crudo* (uncooked).

Quince paste - Made from the quince fruit of a Persian tree. The quince may have been the golden apple of antiquity. Long, slow cooking and generous amounts of sugar bring out the quince's mellow flavor and golden color.

Romesco (rō-METH-kō) - This is a classic Spanish sauce of crushed tomatoes, chiles, garlic, hazelnuts, and almonds, with olive oil and vinegar. It is used for fish.

Rouille (roo-EEY) - This is a firey-flavored, rust-colored sauce of hot chilies, garlic, fresh breadcrumbs, and olive oil pounded into a paste.

Saté (sa-TAY) - This is a dish of cubes of meat, fish, or poultry marinated in a spicy sauce, threaded on skewers, and grilled or broiled. It is Indonesian in origin.

Somen noodles - These are thin white Japanese noodles made from wheat flour. Dried angel hair pasta is a good substitute.

Spiedini (spi-deenee) - This is an Italian term for food grilled on skewers.

Thai fish sauce - Also called Nam Pla, or Nuoc Nam in Vietnam, this is a thin, salty, fermented fish sauce, used as a condiment, sauce, and seasoning ingredient, in much the same way soy sauce is used.

Truffle oil - This is the oil of truffles, which are the fruiting body of a black or white fungus that grows underground.

Velouté (veu-loo-tay) - A stock-based white sauce made from chicken or veal stock or fish fumet thickened with white roux. It is the base for a number of other soups and sauces.

Wakame (wah-kah-mee) - A Japanese seaweed mixture for soups or fresh salads.

Wasabi (wah-sah-bee) - Japanese version of horseradish, although botanically unrelated. It comes fresh, powdered, and as a paste. It is very hot in flavor and green in color.

INDEX

Boldfaced numbers indicate a feature story.

Printed in the USA
CPSIA information can be obtained
at www.ICGtesting.com
LVHW080749050824
787165LV00006B/13